THE LIFE OF A
GOD-MADE MAN

THE LIFE OF A GOD-MADE MAN

Becoming a Man After God's Heart

DAN DORIANI

CROSSWAY BOOKS • WHEATON, ILLINOIS
A DIVISION OF GOOD NEWS PUBLISHERS

Published by Crossway Books
      a division of Good News Publishers
      1300 Crescent Street
      Wheaton, Illinois 60187

Cover design: Cindy Kiple

First printing, 2001

Printed in the United States of America

Library of Congress Cataloging-in-Publication Data
Doriani, Dan, 1953-
    The life of a God-made man / Daniel M. Doriani.
       p. cm.
    Includes bibliographical references and index.
    ISBN 1-58134-308-6 (tpb : alk. paper)
    1. Christian men—Religious life.   I. Title.
BV4528.2 .D67   2001
248.8'42—dc21   2001004879
                                          CIP

15	14	13	12	11	10	09	08	07	06	05	04	03
15	14	13	12	11	10	9	8	7	6	5	4	3

*I dedicate this book to the men of God
at Covenant Seminary, at Kirk of the Hills,
at Central Presbyterian Church,
at the Tuesday morning study and in the
"Things men do" discipleship group.
It has been my joy to teach you these lessons and
to be taught in turn by you.*

TABLE OF CONTENTS

PREFACE

This book is a proposal and a protest. It protests all the books that reduce the life of a Christian man to a string of techniques and how-to lists. It proposes instead that the course of the Christian man is the course of his God. It protests all the lists of four steps for building lasting friendships, five techniques for raising obedient children, and seven methods of loving your wife. To avoid man-made lists, we will spend more time exploring Bible texts than typical men's books do. It also proposes that we focus on character over technique and law. God has renewed His sons and is remaking us in His image. Therefore, it is our heritage, our destiny, to become more like the Father and the Son. Men are most true to themselves when most like Christ.

That conviction shapes this book. Instead of starting with laws and guidelines for godly living, we will consider the nature of God first. For example:

- Godly husbands follow the pattern of sacrificial love set by Jesus, whose love for His bride, the church, shows husbands how to love their wives.

- Good fathers are like God, their heavenly Father. His love, justice, faithfulness, and loving discipline are the pattern for godly fathers.

- Godly friends imitate God's friendship with Abraham and Moses and the friendship of Jesus and His disciples. Self-disclosure and helpful presence are the marks of friendship.

- Godly workers love to create because God, who delights in creation, made us in His image. We like to finish tasks because we resemble Jesus who exulted, "It is finished." His completed mission surpasses all others. But because of Him, we delight in completing our work.

• Even in our play, we imitate the playfulness of God evident throughout creation. His pattern of work and rest liberates us to rest and play as well.

There is more to godly masculinity than this, but nothing is more foundational. God created us in His image. By His grace, He restores us to that image day by day. For that reason I accent character over technique, being over doing.

This approach simply agrees with Jesus. He said, "Every good tree bears good fruit, but a bad tree bears bad fruit. A good tree cannot bear bad fruit, and a bad tree cannot bear good fruit" (Matt. 7:17-18). Jesus says, "I am the vine; you are the branches. If a man remains in me and I in him, he will bear much fruit; apart from me you can do nothing" (John 15:5). Talk of inability offends men who have a high estimate of their strength and resolve. So be it. Progress cannot begin until we know ourselves, weaknesses included. We must know that love, sacrifice, and service are alien to our relentlessly lazy and self-seeking souls. Left to ourselves, we have little desire to sacrifice. But Jesus renews His people.

In the language of Scripture, He gives us a new heart. We have a spiritual sensitivity, even passion. As much as Christian men care about their honor, they care for God's honor yet more. As much as they love their families, they yearn to love their heavenly Father even more. We each become, to borrow another phrase from Scripture, "a man after God's heart."

The phrase "a man after God's heart" was a potential title of this book because it captures the way a changed life radiates out from a renewed spirit. First Samuel 13 used that phrase, long before David became king, to describe him, and it suits him well. He longed for nothing more than God's presence (see Ps. 27). Zeal for God's house consumed him (Ps. 69). This passion of the heart transformed all David did. When a Philistine giant taunted God's people, David could not bear the insult to God's honor and fought him in the Lord's strength (1 Sam. 17). When David became king, his first act was to bring God's tabernacle, the sign of God's presence, into his capital city (2 Sam. 6). As king he showed mercy and protected the weak, such as Mephibosheth (2 Sam. 9), because he knew that God "has regard for the weak [and] delivers him in times of trouble" (Ps. 41:1-2). In the course of his explosive affair with beautiful, reckless Bathsheba, David learned that he was weak too, a man who needed to *receive* mercy and deliverance, not just *give* it (2 Sam. 11). But as a man after God's heart, he eventually confessed his sin to God. Making no excuses, he threw himself on God's mercy, and received it (2 Sam. 12).

The life of David shows that, by themselves, techniques and to-do lists cannot lead anyone to become a man of God. Unless we have a heart for God, techniques only help us manage our lives a little better. Further, if we take our sin, inability, and resistance to repentance seriously, we must conclude that to-do lists will never suffice.

Why then do we act as if we can hand out rules and methods and expect any Joe to follow them? Why do Christian lessons and books sound as if we can solve every problem by following the right techniques? Do they think we can manage every sphere of life if we just have the proper instructions? If so, why are there so many self-help books? Wouldn't three or four be enough to cover most fields of Christian living? Cultures shape people more than the people living in those cultures realize. So I wonder: Do teachers focus on techniques because science, technology, and business dominate our culture? Has our fascination with technology seeped into our theological bones? Have management models led us to think we can govern our relationships by following a few easy steps?

Jesus appears fairly often in some Christian books for men. But He appears as our example more than our Savior. He illustrates the principles of the particular book—the "how-to" of whatever the current chapter requires. But those books say little about Jesus' grace. If they do mention it, it is probably the grace that forgives sins, not the deeper grace that transforms sinners. These books often speak of our sins, but rarely of our sinfulness or our inability to reform ourselves.

Of course, my book will make suggestions about marriage,

fatherhood, money, work, friendship, and play. And I will not ground all of them in the character of God. Some explore the life of faith. Some address Christian discernment, the ability to see things God's way day by day. But the interest in God's character will remain. We become like that which we behold. Technique lists neither motivate nor transform, but the love and grace of God do. When that grace remakes our character into His likeness, it changes all our relationships.

A WORD TO THE WIVES

It is no secret that women like to read men's books on occasion. This is very much a man's book, but I welcome all female readers. After all, women read more than men, who need their beloved to nudge them out of the newspaper into something a bit deeper sometimes. I especially hope husbands and wives will jointly read chapters 3-5, on marriage and parenting. I wrote those chapters for the mouth and the ear, with alliteration and plays on words, so a couple might take pleasure in reading them aloud to each other (making this a read-aloud book?).

ACKNOWLEDGMENTS

I thank Donald Guthrie for taking the mantle of academic administration at Covenant Seminary. Your calling has been my liberation. Thanks to Bryan Stewart for timely and skilled research assistance. You have the knack. Thanks to Debbie for constant encouragement in our journey together. Your laugh is the gift of the year. Special appreciation goes to my colleagues on the faculty at Covenant. Your minds and hearts perpetually enrich mine.

PART 1

THE MAN OF GOD AND HIS LORD

1

A Man after God's heart

About a year ago I experienced downhill skiing for the first time. Each night I instructed a group of men in the Christian faith, and each day they instructed me on the slopes of a peak in the Austrian Alps. I fell down too many times to count; yet the men stuck by me. One gave formal lessons in the morning. Others skied gentler slopes at slower speeds in the afternoon, constantly teaching me their art. On the last run of the fourth afternoon, my companion, an athletic Dutchman, took me to the top of the mountain. "I think you'll like this trail," he said as we hopped off the lift. We skied a short distance and stopped to peer down what looked more like a cliff than a trail.

"That looks a little steep," I said, trying to sound calm.

"Well, yes," my friend replied. "This is where the downhill race starts when the World Cup comes to town."

"How fast do they go?" I wondered aloud.

He pondered for a moment. "About 140 kilometers per hour."

I stared downhill, calculating. "A hundred and forty kilometers is . . . over eighty-five miles an hour."

My friend understood. "It's OK," he assured me. "They go straight down. We'll ski from side to side, across the mountain. Look, I'll go first. Follow in my tracks and you'll be fine." So on that impossibly steep slope, I skied in his tracks. They were the right tracks because they allowed me to ski slowly enough to stay under control and upright (usually) as my skis followed his. Farther down we found milder paths and skied side by side as we enjoyed the mountain's magnificent vistas.

In important ways, the Christian life is like my journey down the mountain. We have to ski the trail, but we're not good enough. Left to our own devices, we will fall down over and over. Left to our own devices, we will die. But we are not on our own. Someone is willing to help us find the right path down the mountain. At the deepest level, that someone is God, our helper. At another level, our fellow Christian men help us. They know the way down. They have negotiated the path with skill, skiing the trail beforehand, making a track for us to follow.

The Christian life is somewhat like skiing in the right path. Moses called the people of God to "walk in all his ways" (Deut. 11:22). Similarly, Paul says Christians should "walk in the footsteps of the faith that our father Abraham had" (Rom. 4:12). The Christian life is a walk, a journey in the right path. Yet, to be a man after God's own heart, we must understand the journey correctly. Specifically, while skiing and walking are athletic images, we do not achieve success as Christians merely by our skillful striving. We must beware of Christianity as performance, or what I call Nike Christianity.

FOLLOWING THE PATH OF PERFORMANCE— NIKE CHRISTIANITY

Performance Christianity, or Nike Christianity, is a "just do it" approach to the Christian life. Nike Christianity is a form of legalism. Like hepatitis, legalism is a disease with several forms. Legalism A, the most deadly, believes that we can *do* something to obtain salvation, to *earn* God's favor (think of the rich young man in Matthew 19). Legalism B requires believers to submit to man-made commandments as if they were the Law of God (think of the Pharisees). Legalism C, Nike Christianity, thinks of Christian living as little more than obedience to the *Law* of God, minimizing or neglecting our *relationship* with God. It reasons, "God says we should tithe; so tithe. The Bible says we must pray; so pray. It says submit to leaders, witness, read Scripture; so we should submit, witness, and read. Just do it." Some Christian leaders, often unintentionally, support Nike Christianity. One said, "The moral keynote of Christianity must be obedience." It is "submission to demands," so that "God calls and man obeys."[1] Of course, Christians must obey God. But obedience is not the essence of Christian living, as we shall see.

A great deal of Christian literature for men smacks of Nike Christianity. Books stress the need to repent, to start living better, according to the advice the authors dispense. Nike Christian literature loves how-to lists. It offers five ways to form edifying friendships, six pointers for handling conflict, seven steps toward exercising loving leadership, and eight techniques for more effective parenting.

Nike speakers set up their advice by reciting litanies of woes afflicting our culture. Next they ask how we can break the downward spiral. Their answer goes roughly like this: We break the cycle by getting men to assume their responsibilities. If anyone has failed, he needs to confess his sins to God. Then, O man, "Recommit yourself to your spiritual priorities. Get back on your feet, dust yourself off, and 'go and sin no more.'"[2] In essence, such talks or books go like this:

• Some of you are doing bad things. You should stop it! God wants you to do good things instead of bad things.

• Some of you are doing good things. Keep it up!

• Here is how to keep it up: You must plan to endure, taking these steps: Make a decision. Pray every morning. Commit yourself to God 100 percent. Avoid temptation. Guard your mind, heart, and eyes. Seek an accountability partner. Then you will stay on the right path.

THE PROBLEM WITH NIKE CHRISTIANITY

In a way, no one can object to this advice; those who dispense it certainly mean well. But the relentless stress on what men should *do* misses the most basic issue: the heart issue. Men fail to take the steps to do what they should because they don't *want* to take those steps. Pray regularly? Some men know they should but fail because they have no desire to be alone with God in prayer. They fear Him more than they love Him. Commit ourselves to God 100 percent? We are double-minded, resisting God's authority one hour and embracing it the next. Seek accountability? Many men *avoid* accountability because they prefer to answer to themselves alone. They don't want to guard their mind or eye too closely. They *want* to indulge the eye's lusts for women and the mind's fantasies of dominance or wealth.

Yes, most popular Christian books geared to men or women, and most books about marriage and family, have a strong whiff of Nike Christianity. They are full of advice, but nearly devoid of grace. They speak often of what we should do for God, but little of what God has done for us. They often invoke the *example* of Jesus but rarely discuss the *prior love* of Jesus that draws us to love Him.

One day I was reading such a book in our family room as my wife sat nearby. The author was telling women how to act so their husbands would love them and long for their company: They must never nag. They must never greet their beleaguered heroes at the door with a litany of the day's problems. Rather they must always be welcoming, gentle, thankful, complimentary. Never criticize, complain, or get angry, the author said. Then your husband will love your very presence.

Not a bad book, I thought at first. But as the obligations heaped up, I began to wonder what a real woman would say to this. So, selecting the lead sentences in fifteen or twenty sections, I read the gist of it to my wife. After five minutes or so, I paused, "What do you think?"

"It's good advice," she said thoughtfully. "But I felt overwhelmed and defeated after the first five ideas—and there were a dozen more." Exactly. What else can we say about books that tell us, in the final analysis, "Your husband [or your wife] will love you more if you never make a mistake."

Please understand—it is good to submit to God's Law and to follow Jesus' example. The Savior is also our Sovereign and Lord (Jude

4). The Creator and Redeemer has all authority in Heaven and on earth. Our sins grieve God, and He delights in our obedience, an obedience we owe Him. But obedience is just one element of the Christian life, not its essence. Furthermore, obedience is neither the root nor the highest fruit of Christian living.

From the beginning, God's love and grace has always come before His demands. As John says, "We love because he [God] first loved us" (1 John 4:19). As Paul says, the love of Christ, who died for us, compels us to live, not for ourselves, but for God (2 Cor. 5:14-15). As Paul also says, it is "the *grace* of God," not the *Law* of God, that "teaches us to say 'No' to ungodliness and worldly passions" (Titus 2:11-12). Commands don't change people—love does. Unless God first loves a man and reconciles that man to Himself, that person cannot obey God's commands.

If we tell an atheist, "Store up for yourselves treasures in Heaven," he will not and cannot, for the command is nonsense to him. If he believes there is no God in Heaven, why should he plan for it?

If we tell a teenager who despises her mother, "You must respect your mother," she cannot do so. She cannot *show* respect if she does not *have* respect. She may obey her mother, but she will do it grudgingly, with rolling eyes and slouching shoulders. She needs a changed relationship with her mother—a change of heart.

Similarly, it makes little sense to tell a godless man to stop sinning. We might as well command a drowning man to swim. It is true that the drowning man needs to swim, but the problem is that he cannot. Likewise, a man who has decided to make his happiness, career, and appetites his gods will not and *cannot* obey a command to put others first. He neither can do it, nor does he wish to do so. As Paul says, "The sinful mind is hostile to God. It does not submit to God's law, nor can it do so" (Rom. 8:7).

The Law has very important roles. It labels sin and shows people their sinfulness. It promotes civil order and reins in our wilder impulses. It states what we owe to others, and especially to God. Because every one of His commands reflects God's character, the

Law shows us how to grow in conformity to Him. But the Law, by itself, cannot change the heart.

THE ROOT OF A GODLY LIFE

I recently spoke to a Christian businessman who has a passion for discipleship. Frustrated by his slow progress with a few men, he asked me, "Dan, tell me, how do you get people to change? Where do they get the *ability* to change? How can I get them"—he was punctuating every word—"to do . . . *what's* . . . *right?*" Because my friend has started, through the power of God's grace, to break free from Nike Christianity, he was ready for my reply: "Commands can change the behavior of children or employees, if you have the ability to punish disobedience. But law, by itself, never renews the heart. Only the love and grace of God can change us. The truth changes people if they are receptive, if the Spirit has given them 'ears to hear.' But teachers do not have the power to change men. At most, we can expose them to God's Word. *We* cannot 'make' people do what is right."

Who can? Jeremiah said Israel would change when God gave His people a soft, fleshy heart to replace their heart of stone (Ezek. 11:19; 36:26; cf. Jer. 31:33-34). Jesus said the secrets of the kingdom were given to some but taken from others (Matt. 13:11-15). Paul said the preaching of the Gospel of Christ is foolishness unless God's Spirit grants the ability to understand truths that are spiritually discerned (1 Cor. 1:21—2:14). In short, the *root* of obedience is God's prior grace, and the *fruit* of obedience is conformity to His person and His plans. As Jerry Bridges says:

> Now the fact is we do have a duty and obligation to God. He is the Sovereign Ruler of this world, and in that capacity, He has "laid down precepts that are to be fully obeyed" (Psalm 119:4). But He motivates us to obedience, not on the basis of His sovereign rule, but on the basis of His mercy to us in Jesus Christ. . . . I am committed to seek to act in love toward everyone. But I am committed in these areas out of a grateful response to God's grace, not to try to earn God's blessings.[3]

That is a gospel principle. We do not produce good works in order to acquire God's love, but because we have His love. Everything hangs on the conjunctions. We obey not *in order to* obtain God's salvation, but *because* God already saved us. Scripture motivates obedience by describing God's prior love. At Sinai, before declaring the Law, God reminded Israel of His covenant-making love:

> *"You yourselves have seen what I did to Egypt, and how I carried you on eagles' wings and brought you to myself. Now if you obey me fully and keep my covenant, then out of all nations you will be my treasured possession . . . a kingdom of priests and a holy nation. . . . I am the LORD your God, who brought you out of Egypt, out of the land of slavery. You shall have no other gods before me."*
>
> —EXOD. 19:4-6; 20:2-3

So God's grace enables and impels us to live for Him. Yet, there are ways to think about obedience that partially detach it from the principles of covenant and grace. Like so many others, I experienced this very detachment for a number of years.

THE MOTIVES FOR A GODLY LIFE

When I was a new Christian, my teachers clearly taught the lordship of Christ. They showed the importance of obedience in every sphere of life. Yet, my thinking was somewhat muddled as to why I obeyed. If asked to explain, I answered three ways, which I call the way of wisdom, the way of trust, and the way of gratitude.

The way of wisdom says, "It is only reasonable to obey God's Law. After all, He created all things, so He knows how they work. Therefore, we expect His commands to be effective, to bring us good." As Moses said (Deut. 10:12-13), "And now, O Israel, what does the LORD your God ask of you but to fear the LORD your God, to walk in all his ways, to love him, to serve the LORD your God with all your heart and with all your soul, and to observe the LORD's com-

mands and decrees that I am giving you today for your own good?"
If God gives His commands for our good, then it only makes sense
to obey commands that will prove to be "good" for us.

The way of trust believes God loves us and would never mislead
us. We should behave as He directs and trust Him to make it work.
If we do what is right for Him, He will do what is right for us.

The way of gratitude judges that it is fitting for us to obey God
without reserve because God first gave Himself without reserve to
us when He redeemed us. Because He has done so much for us, we
should be willing to do much for Him.

These perspectives on obedience grasp profound truths. They
are certainly superior to the way of merit, where people obey God to
earn or retain His favor. And they surpass the way of fear, where people obey God to avert punishment. It is always good to obey God's
Law, but He cannot be pleased with anyone who obeys Him only to
merit rewards or avoid penalties. Such "obedience" is entirely selfish, even manipulative, and has no love of God in it.

Yet, if we pause, we see that those walking in the ways of wisdom, trust, and gratitude partially obey for God's sake and partially
for selfish reasons. There is trust and gratitude toward the Lord, but
there is also a desire to gain benefits and to relieve debts. Thus these
motives fall short of the noblest purpose for obedience: the desire to
obey God for His sake alone, out of love for Him. Of course, when
we love God, blessings follow, but we love God for His sake, not simply to receive favors from Him.

Bernard of Clairvaux, the great pastor and theologian of the
twelfth century, put it this way: We cajole the unwilling with promises
and rewards, not the willing. Who offers men rewards for doing
what they want to do? Do we pay hungry men to eat? Do we pay
thirsty men to drink? So, Bernard says, if we demand a reward to
obey God, we love the reward rather than God.[4] In his words, "The
soul that loves God seeks no other reward than that God whom it
loves. Were the soul to demand anything else, then it would certainly
love that other thing and not God."[5]

To illustrate, suppose three men go running five days each

week. Suppose, further, that we ask each one why he is so dedicated to running.

The first answers, "I run because my father died of a heart attack at fifty-one, and I want to live long enough to retire and to see my grandchildren grow up."

The second replies, "I run so I can eat anything I want and still not gain weight. Running also makes me tired enough to sleep soundly at night."

The third says, "When I run, my legs soar over the ground, the wind brushes my face, my heart beats like slow, heavy thunder in my chest, and I feel *alive*."

The first man runs out of fear; he is afraid of what will happen if he stops. The second runs for its benefits. He runs because it enhances the quality of his life; he eats and sleeps better. For the third man, running is its own reward. The first and second men love health and food and sleep. Running is an instrument they use to gain what they desire. Only the third man actually loves running in itself.

The obedience of many Christians resembles the first two runners. They obey in order to avoid what they fear or to gain what they desire. Only a few serve God seeking, above all else, God Himself. Ideally, then, the man after God's heart loves the Lord for *His* sake. Yet, we love God as He reveals Himself in history and in the Bible. We love God for His grace and for His Gospel. The idea of loving God for His own sake is daunting to most of us. And of course because He is so generous, and because His generosity precedes our faith, it is hard to separate God from His blessings. So the Lord does not expect us to "work up" love for Him. Rather, by revealing His love and grace, He draws us to Himself.

KNOWING GRACE

Sadly, it is harder to appreciate God's grace today than it was a few decades ago, because no one seems to be guilty of anything anymore. People have guilt feelings, but no guilt. Everyone is a victim, but no one seems to be a victimizer, unless they are already victims themselves. Rarely does anyone do anything that they admit to be *wrong*.

The story of Katherine Powers is a case in point. A radical student protester who attended Brandeis University in the 1960s, Powers committed several crimes in 1969. To start a revolution aimed at overthrowing the United States government, Powers helped rob a bank. The money would buy explosives to derail a Defense Department train carrying weapons that would be diverted to the Black Panthers, who would start an armed rebellion.

During the robbery, a policeman, a father of nine, responded to the silent alarm. An ex-convict, serving as a lookout across the street, unloaded his submachine gun into the officer's back, killing him, leaving behind a widow and nine children. Powers was no naive schoolgirl briefly carried along by a charismatic leader. Investigators later found a large store of weapons and ammunition in her apartment. Powers fled the scene and eluded the FBI, who put her on their "ten most wanted" list for fourteen years.

Powers moved to Oregon, became Alice Metzinger, had a son, got married, became a gourmet chef, and hid her past. Then in 1992 she became depressed, sleepless, and suicidal. She decided she had to get her life back; she had to become Katherine Powers again. To do that she had to turn herself in to the authorities, which she did in 1993. We might possibly applaud this, until we hear what she said about her crimes when she surrendered herself: "I was naive and unthinking. . . . I never intended to hurt anybody."

When someone asked why she turned herself in, she replied, "I know that I must answer this accusation from the past in order to live with full authenticity in the present." In case this was unclear, her husband explained, "She did not return out of guilt. She was tired of telling lies. She wanted her life back. She wanted her truth back. She wanted to be whole." Powers did not return to repent, to apologize, to pay a debt to society, or to make amends to the policeman's widow and children. She did it for therapeutic reasons, to recover herself. In such an atmosphere, it is no wonder that pastors sometimes feel like buggy whip salesmen, offering a product nobody wants.

There could hardly be a greater contrast than that between the guilt-deniers, illustrated by Powers, and biblical Christianity, illustrated by the apostle Paul. Guilt-deniers reject the idea that they ever did anything wrong. If they did, it was long ago and unintentional, when they were a different person. But over thirty years after his conversion, after decades of ceaseless labor and suffering for Christ, Paul still did not excuse his sin. Rather, he said, "Christ Jesus came into the world to save sinners—of whom I am the worst." Notice that he did not say, "I *was* the worst." He neither distanced himself from nor denied his past, when he blasphemed Christ and persecuted the church. He admitted his sin plainly and advertised it as proof that no one is beyond the pale of God's grace (1 Tim. 1:15-16).

David's worst hour proves that this grace even covers sins committed after we come to faith. Before introducing David to Samuel, God told Samuel he was seeking "a man after his own heart" (1 Sam. 13:14), one who would succeed Saul as king. Indeed, David became Israel's shepherd-king, strong yet merciful and zealous for God. His passion for God proved itself when he first appeared to face Goliath in single combat. His heart for God showed right after his coronation when, in his first regal act, he brought the ark of the covenant to Jerusalem. No wonder David became the measure for all kings to follow. Yet, in one outburst of sin with Bathsheba, this best king broke all ten commandments (2 Sam. 11). We see the scope of his sin by working backward through the Decalogue:

- #10: His sin began when he coveted Bathsheba, another man's wife.
- #9: He deceived that man (Uriah) in his attempt to cover up Bathsheba's pregnancy.
- #7, 8: He stole Uriah's wife and committed adultery with her.
- #6: When his cover-up failed, he arranged Uriah's death by exposing him and his men to murderous enemy fire in battle.
- #5: David's sin dishonored his parents. What parent would not be ashamed if their children did what David did?

- #1-3: In all of this, David followed another god, making his desires into his idol and serving them, so that the name of the Lord, whom he professed to serve, was put to shame.
- #4: David desecrated the Sabbath by remaining impenitent for a year. Every Sabbath his worship was a hypocritical lie as he hid his sin and refused God's remedy.

All this David did deliberately, callously, from a public position. By the Law, David deserved to die for such sins. Yet God showed him mercy. He sent the prophet Nathan to rebuke the king through an irresistible parable (2 Sam. 12:1-7), ending with the accusation to David, "You are the man!"

When charged, David responded simply, "I have sinned against the LORD" (12:13). He offered no extenuating circumstances ("You can't imagine how my regular wives have been acting recently"), no excuses ("All the other kings do it"), no blame-shifting ("She was bathing in plain sight"). He did not say, "I have sinned, but . . ." He simply admitted his sin, with a mere three words in the original.[6] He didn't even beg for mercy. He simply admitted his guilt and labeled it sin against the Lord.

Nathan's reply was just as terse: "The LORD has taken away your sin" (12:13b). David would bear consequences for his sin (his son would die), but God's mercy carries no contingencies or conditions. Nathan did not say, "You will be forgiven if you prove you are sorry" or "You will have to do something to make up for this." David's sins deserved death, but he repented and God forgave him. No sin stands outside the perimeter of divine grace.

David's poems celebrating God's mercy entered the Bible's book of worship songs as Psalms 32 and 51. "The sacrifices of God are a broken spirit; a broken and contrite heart, O God, you will not despise" (Ps. 51:17). In Romans, when Paul decides to illustrate the long reach of God's amazing grace, he makes David the spokesman, the paradigm, "of the blessedness of the man to whom God credits righteousness apart from works: 'Blessed are they whose transgressions are forgiven, whose sins are covered. Blessed is the man whose sin the Lord will never count against him'" (4:6-8).

The man after God's heart is a sinner, and everywhere he goes, he participates in societies of sinners. At work he puts down his rivals; he shades the truth to get a slight advantage. At home he rebukes his children a little too harshly for sins *he* showed them how to commit. With a friend, he puts up an argument even when he knows he is wrong, because he would rather *be* wrong than *appear* to be wrong. In athletic contests and in checkout lines, he chooses not to correct errors made in his favor. He would weep over it all if he were not so cold. *I know it; at least I know it*, we think. We cling to the Gospel, but even our clinging is tainted because we are too glad that our sin is covered, and not sorry enough that we did it. We even need to repent of our repentance. We are aware that our faith lines up a little off-kilter too. But is that realization good or bad? The realization is good, but being off-kilter is bad. Yet there is more good than bad in the situation because saving faith rests not on the *quality* of the faith but on the *object* of the faith. God even saves us from the defects in our faith. The man after God's heart knows this and so returns again and again to the beloved Gospel.

LOVING THE GOSPEL

Men after God's heart return to the Gospel because they know they forget the Gospel. Even ministers of the Gospel neglect the Gospel. The New Testament shows that even the apostles sometimes forgot the Gospel, as we see in an oddly comforting episode from the life of Peter.

In Acts 10, God welcomed a Roman centurion named Cornelius into the family of God by faith alone, without works, without giving up his Gentile heritage. God chose Peter to preach the Gospel to Cornelius, a "God-fearing" Gentile (v. 2), but Peter had a hard time accepting it.[7] Before Peter would be willing to go to Cornelius, God had to send him a vision of a sheet lowered from Heaven, holding all kinds of clean and unclean animals. Three times God said, "Rise, Peter, kill and eat." Three times Peter refused: "Surely not, Lord! I have never eaten anything impure or unclean." And three times a voice from Heaven said, "Do not call anything impure that God has made clean" (vv. 11-16). While Peter wondered what this might mean, Cornelius' servants arrived at Peter's house, seeking him. Peter had no idea who they were, but the Spirit told Peter, "Do not hesitate to go with them" (vv. 17-22). Peter must have been shocked when he found that the men were Gentiles, but he obeyed and went. When Peter arrived at Cornelius' house, a crowd of Gentiles awaited him. When Peter greeted them, he told them God had sent him. Then he asked, "May I ask why you sent for me?" (vv. 24-29).

When I read this question, I want to laugh and tell him, "Peter, you are an apostle, a herald of the Gospel! Surely you know why God sent you there!" But Cornelius did not laugh. Instead he urged Peter to present his message: "It was good of you to come. Now we are all here in the presence of God to listen to everything the Lord has commanded you to tell us" (v. 33).

Then Peter began to preach: "I now realize how true it is that God does not show favoritism but accepts men from every nation who fear him and do what is right" (vv. 34-35). Again I want to laugh at Peter, to shake him. "Peter, how can you say, 'I *now* realize.' Surely you knew before. You saw Jesus heal Gentiles, talk to Samaritans, and purge demoniacs from Gadara or Phoenicia (Matt. 15; John 4; Luke 8). How can you say, 'I *now* realize God accepts people from every nation'? Surely you already knew that!"

We laugh at Peter. Yet like Peter, we know and we don't know. We know the Gospel, but we need to grasp it more deeply, more truly. We all have moments when we think, *Now* I realize; now *I understand the Gospel.*

Let me speak personally. My father belongs to the unexpressive generation, the Stoics who grew up in the Depression, World War II, and its aftermath. I know my father loves me, but for many years he never said, "I love you, son." I knew he was proud of me, but he could not say it directly. His generation seldom praised its children for fear of spoiling them. Men raised by such fathers often have an odd blend of two traits. On one hand, we are confident and self-sufficient; we despise flattery. On the other hand, we yearn for praise from our fathers. Something in us wants to be so good that they will *have* to say, "I love you." We want to do something so great that they will be compelled to say, "I am proud of you." But our fathers may not be able to say that. Our fathers may even be dead. So what will happen to our desperate longing for the words, "I love you, I accept you, I am proud of you"?

Our cure is in the Gospel, for the Gospel proclaims a Father who loved us when we ignored Him, cursed Him, and ran from Him. He loves all His children, including all whose fathers and mothers never said, "I love you. I am proud of you." His love is free, unconditional. There is nothing we can do to make Him love us more than He already does. Indeed, when we alienated ourselves from Him, He pursued us and reconciled us to Himself in love. More, he adopted us as His children; He welcomed us into His family. Jesus is now our older brother. In Heaven, Jesus points to us in pride and announces, "Here am I, and the children God has given me" (Heb. 2:11-13).

Sadly, Christians get tired of the Gospel. The Gospel itself is not boring, of course. The problem is that we repeat the briefest form of the Gospel—"Jesus died for our sins; believe in Him and be saved"— almost mindlessly. But if we meditate upon the Gospel, we see that while it meets our deepest spiritual needs, it also meets our emotional needs. So for everyone who seeks a father's praise, the Gospel says, "Stop striving. God loves you and accepts you without a performance, without conditions." The Gospel liberates us in more ways as well.

- *Justification cures the guilt and condemnation of sin.* It releases all who suffer from self-condemnation. God, the Judge, has justified us in Christ. Who are we to condemn ourselves (Rom. 8:33-34)?
- *Reconciliation removes the alienation of sin.* God has made peace with Him, has given us peace, and peace in the church. Now we need not wonder if we belong, or if anyone loves us.
- *Redemption liberates us from the power of sin.* Jesus delivered us from captivity to sin, death, and the devil. However we may feel, we are no longer trapped by sin.

• *Jesus' propitiation put aside God's just wrath toward our sins.* His love for us and our love for Him cast out servile fear.[8]

At each point the Gospel meets heart-felt needs. At each point people should say with Peter, "Now I realize! Now I understand the Gospel!" no matter how familiar it seems.

LIVING AS A MAN AFTER GOD'S HEART

Scan the shelves of most Christian bookstores and you will see that how-to books dominate the field. They stress rules, techniques, methods, and keys to success rather than grace and the Gospel. They roll out lists of things men should do to please their wives, control their tempers, nurture their children, and find inner peace, all guaranteed by successful Christian businessmen, athletes, and leaders. If Jesus appears, He probably functions as an example, not as the Savior. The apostles are also primarily examples rather than fellow-heirs of salvation.

I once heard a talk on Peter's denial of Christ that went like this: Peter's life had a lot of ups and downs, just like ours. Peter's denial of Christ shows that "our reach often exceeds our grasp; we all fail sometimes." But like Peter, we can get up and start over, if we know how to proceed. The advice that followed was sound but misleading, because the implicit message was, "You can do it." *But we cannot.*

To live as men after God's heart, we need more than good advice. We need deliverance. We need God to change us. To return to the opening illustration, we don't need skiing tips—we need the ability to ski. We need God to remake us in His image. We are sinners created in the image of God and recreated in the image of Christ. Because Christian living begins and ends with God, techniques and how-to advice can never be primary. Because we are sinners, Christ's redemption comes first. Because our goal is conformity to the image of Christ (Rom. 8:29), He also goes last. That will be the focus of this book. We will often return to grace and our re-creation in the image of Christ. But first we need to understand our culture's images of masculinity, images that can blind us to the image of *godly* masculinity.

Discussion Questions

1. Why does legalism appeal to almost every Christian at some time? To what extent are you a "Just Do It" Christian? What is the cure for legalism?

2. How do people change? How have you answered that question in the past? How do you answer it now?

3. List all the motives people can have for obeying God. What are your main motives for living as a disciple? How might you move to higher motives?

4. How do you handle your sin? Are you a guilt denier? Why is it hard to confess your sins? What makes it easier to confess them? Do you need to confess any sins to God or others?

5. Do you sometimes forget the Gospel? Why? Do you believe the cure for many fundamental problems is found in the Gospel? List some "heart problems" people have. How does the Gospel cure them?

2

IMAGES OF MANHOOD

Boys get ideas about manhood in the oddest places. I found my first concept of masculinity in a doctor's office. As a little boy, I was active but short, slender, and often sick. Looking back, I now see that the members of my family, who all valued toughness, wondered if little Danny would make the grade. The doctor set the defining moments in motion when he decided I should receive shots for the allergies that weakened me, starting at the tender age of four. First came diagnostic "scratch tests" in which the doctor hooked a curved, antigen-tipped needle through the skin on my back, piercing it twice, then withdrawing it. Little as I was, I lay silent and motionless—for all ninety-six needles! Afterward I received five to seven shots per week for several years.

For whatever reason, I was a "very good boy" through my torment, never whimpering or complaining. My bravery became legendary with doctors and nurses, who soon decided I could be useful. When I was in the office and an older boy wept or quailed at the prospect of shots, the doctor would wave me into his presence, calling out, "Nurse, bring in exhibit A. He knows how brave boys act." The nurses led me into the needle corral and drew serum into rapier-like syringes, while seven- and nine-year-olds endured the humiliation of watching a wraith-like four-year-old endure the pain with a cool that boasted, "Bring on your needles! Do your worst. I fear you not."

My parents told the story for decades, for I had passed a test of masculinity. Whatever my size or health, my bravery became, for my family, a badge of my toughness, my true masculinity. My ego would like to cling to this, but sometimes I wonder if I am truly brave or if I just have poor nerve endings. More important, what exactly does the ability to endure physical pain have to do with true masculinity? Is tough-minded suffering a *biblical* measure of manliness? Or is it merely cultural?

We live in a day marked by competing concepts of true manhood. Are real men hard or soft? Are diapers and dishes beneath their dignity, or are they so secure they can plunge their hands into those waters? Do true men bear pain, physical and emotional, in impressive, impassive silence, or are they so self-assured that they shed tears openly and speak of it freely? Do real men provide for their families, keeping food on the table even if they have to manage two jobs and earning heaps of money if they can? Or are they so confident of their skills and values that they will walk away from a good-paying but stifling job, knowing they can get another, and believing it better to have less with integrity than to have more with compromise? Going a bit deeper, does virtue have gender? Is the greatest man almost identical, in character, behavior, and roles, to the greatest woman? Or does the form of greatness shift when the gender changes?

Anyone who wants to read this book is old enough to have pulled a few models of masculinity off the rack. They seem to fit at first but later pinch in one place and billow out foolishly in another. Once they show their poor design, we want to toss out these defective notions and move on without further thought. But our friends, families, and society still find them workable—and we do too, on some days. So we had better look at a few of them: the tough guy, the good provider, the soft man, and the self-actualized man.

THE TOUGH GUY

"Tough guy" was the first model of masculinity that my small mind absorbed. Adults say, "Big boys don't cry," and some children believe that deep within themselves. At the doctor's office I made first proof of my masculinity. Other men get tough guy reputations through fights in alleys or in business suites, through battles in military uniforms or in athletic uniforms. Millions of men have breathed the air of the tough guy model of masculinity as they grew up. They became traditional men who ruled the military and the business world, at least until the 1980s. Traditional tough men get up early, work hard, admire discipline, provide for their families, sacrifice for others, and love their country. They know their responsibilities, but they may not know their heart, or the heart of their wives, children, or friends (if they have any friends). They cannot cry. They choke on phrases like, "I love you." They are dutiful and strong, but their strength is one-dimensional. They probably are not good communicators or mentors, and probably not warm husbands or fathers. This leads us to a basic question: Is the tough guy code of quiet sacrifice and quiet emotions valid? Is it biblical?

Actually, it is commendable to be tough enough to endure physical pain. Endurance is a biblical virtue, and the ability to persevere through suffering is an indispensable part of it. Certainly believers should remain faithful in times of persecution, and that requires a willingness to endure fear and pain. The New Testament compares Christian living to athletic struggle, to a race, to boxing (1 Cor. 9:24-27; 2 Tim. 2:5; Heb. 12:1-4), activities that demand endurance and entail suffering. Likewise, traditional male activities such as waging war and performing manual labor require men to suppress their awareness of pain. Of course, the waging of war keeps getting cleaner (not to say easier) as we fire at targets dozens of miles distant. Work gets easier (physically, at least) too as more men work with computers than with hand tools. Still, the sense remains that men must provide for and protect their families despite pain. In fact, Scripture assumes that men will toil and defend their nation.

Jesus models virtuous toughness in three ways: 1) He finished arduous tasks. 2) He waged war and prevailed. 3) He defied pain for the sake of others. First, Jesus finished the task of redemption by offering Himself as atonement for sin on the cross (Matt. 20:25-28;

John 19:30). Second, He entered solo combat against His "family's" great foe and defeated Him. He tied up the strong man because He was stronger (Matt. 12:29). He crushed the head of the ancient serpent and defeated him forever (Gen. 3:15; Rev. 20:2-3). He defeated the agent of death (Heb. 2:14-15). He silenced the accuser (Rev. 12:9-10). Third, Jesus endured intense suffering, even death, death on a cross; but He scorned the pain and shame in order to achieve His goals (Phil. 2:5-8; Heb. 12:2-3). Scripture presents Jesus, in all this toughness and sacrifice for others, as an example to us. Notice the phrases that mark Jesus as our example:

> *Whoever wants to become great among you must be your servant, and whoever wants to be first must be your slave—just as the Son of Man did not come to be served, but to serve, and to give his life as a ransom for many.*
>
> —MATT. 20:26-28

> *Your attitude should be the same as that of Christ Jesus: Who, being in very nature God, did not consider equality with God something to be grasped, but made himself nothing, taking the very nature of a servant, being made in human likeness. And being found in appearance as a man, he humbled himself and became obedient to death—even death on a cross.*
>
> —PHIL. 2:5-8

> *Let us fix our eyes on Jesus, the author and perfecter of our faith, who for the joy set before him endured the cross, scorning its shame, and sat down at the right hand of the throne of God. Consider him who endured such opposition from sinful men, so that you will not grow weary and lose heart.*
>
> —HEB. 12:2-3

There is, therefore, more to the tough guy model of masculinity than we might first think. Yet the tough guy persona has unbiblical elements that hurt men in several ways. A hyper-traditional, John Wayne model of toughness says men are tough, independent, self-controlled, self-governing, self-contained. Such men say, "I'm tough, and I don't need no help from nobody." The tough guy model may promote endurance, but it also promotes a kind of silence that suppresses honest self-disclosure. It encourages men to keep their troubles to themselves and to solve them on their own or to suffer in silence, because that's what they think real men do. It fosters the evasive language many men use to talk about their troubles, so that we have to decode it.

- "Things have been a little rough at home" might mean, "My wife has hired a divorce lawyer."
- "I'm not the husband I should be" might mean, "I work eighty hours a week and throw raging fits every few days."
- "I should give more attention to my children" might mean, "I'm not sure I remember how old they are right now."

Tough guy thinking denies fundamental Christian ideas. The tough guy says, "I can solve all my problems," but the Bible says we cannot. The tough guy says, "I am self-sufficient," but God says we are not. The tough guy says, "I don't need help from anybody," but the Bible says we can never meet our greatest needs in our own strength.

Men with such a lifelong pattern will do some things and have some attitudes that please God. Still, if a man tries to live by the John Wayne, tough guy model of masculinity alone, he will find it difficult to grow as a Christian. I am not going to plead with you to "get in touch with your feelings" (whatever that means). But the tough guy is too self-contained, too pinched emotionally to build strong open relationships with family or friends. And without solid relationships, he may be susceptible to other faulty models of masculinity, beginning with the provider model.

THE GOOD PROVIDER

The good provider is a cousin of the tough guy. The good provider believes he is responsible to get married and to provide a comfortable life for his family. The good provider liberates his wife to be a homemaker, to cook and clean, to decorate and entertain, to volunteer in the community, to organize schedules, and generally to make their home a haven in a heartless world. The good provider strides into the world, slaying dragons, cutting deals, and moving tons of rocks for his family's sake. He brings home the bacon, and his wife cooks it up. The reward is admiration, but the price is pressure to produce, even if that means endless labor and mindless conformity to the world of gray suits, blue collars, or business casual. The good provider works hard to provide financially, but he gets home so tired and so low as the last bit of adrenaline wears off that he cannot provide emotionally. Again, is this notion of manhood biblical or cultural?

As with the tough guy, Scripture commends parts of the good provider model. First, Scripture always assumes and sometimes commands that men work to provide for their families. From the beginning, before the Fall, Adam worked God's garden and kept it. The patriarchs all worked, tending flocks and herds. Many of Moses' laws protect the rights and lives of farmers. Jesus was a carpenter and could probably build with stone as well. Paul was a tent-maker who was glad to work with his hands lest he be a burden to anyone. Further, he forbade idleness and ordered early Christians to work lest they prove to be a burden (1 Thess. 2:7-9; 2 Thess. 3:6-11). As he said, "If anyone is not willing to work, then he is not to eat, either" (2 Thess. 3:10).

In addition to these examples and commands, God Himself models the good provider role. God is our Father, and as a husband of Israel He provided well for her. He bestowed wealth on the patriarchs Abraham, Isaac, Jacob, and Joseph. After delivering Israel from Egypt, He fed her food from Heaven called manna when she wandered in the wilderness. God also gave wealth to David and Solomon and other good kings (1 Kings 10; 1 Chron. 28—29) and even to the common folk of Israel (Ps. 128). As provider, David also compared God to a good shepherd who leads the flock to green pastures and quiet waters (Ps. 23). Indeed, Psalm 104 shows that God provides for the earth and all its birds and beasts. And Jesus is a good provider as well, not only materially but in delivering and protecting His people.

So the good provider model has biblical roots. A good man *does* provide for his family. Yet men can distort the good provider model in ways that make it more cultural than biblical. For example, we often misquote Paul's words in 1 Timothy 5:8, making him say, "If a *man* does not provide for his family, he is worse than an unbeliever." But the apostle actually says, "If *anyone* does not provide for his relatives, and especially for his immediate family, he has denied the faith and is worse than an unbeliever." In its original context, Paul sought to ensure that men care for widows and other poor relatives, not just their wives and children. Furthermore, the word translated "provide" does not mean "earn" or "acquire" but to "plan" or "look out" for something. That is, Paul does not require men to *earn* all the money. Rather, men must ensure that the family *has* all the money it needs.[1] It is fine, therefore, for a woman to earn money. After all, the noble woman of Proverbs 31 sells garments and real estate. Moreover, there is no law against a woman earning more than her husband (though it may cause tensions). Certainly a man fulfills his obligations if he plans for his wife to earn most of their income for a few years while he receives training for a job that will provide their livelihood for decades.

The good provider image harbors dangers too. First, it promotes the idea that a man is what he earns. It pushes us to conform to our acquisitive culture, which judges gaining and spending to be the essence of the good life. Second, the accent on earning pushes men to work long hours and to shove relations with family and friends aside. Third, the good provider syndrome can contribute to the dark side of mobility and rootlessness. To pursue higher income, men must be willing to move to another city or state to get higher salaries. As we haul anchor and sail away from relatives and friends, we lose contact with people who know the best and worst of who we are. When we sever the cords of family or local church history and tradition, we distance ourselves from people who share stories about sweet babies, terrible storms, and great contests. I will not even mention the consequences for our wives and children.

Good providers are by no means a rare breed, but like tough

guys, they are a more traditional kind of men. But other models of masculinity are also emerging.

THE SOFTER MAN

The softer man is a thoughtful, gentle breed.[2] He is a sweet nurturer more than fierce protector. He takes pride in changing diapers and doing dishes alongside his wife. There are no guns in his house. The softer man will lift weights, but he will not play football or other contact sports. He is empathetic more than flinty. He can feel your pain, but he may not know how to remove it. He says, "I feel so sorry for you," not "Buck up; it's time to get back to work." When he meets resistance, he becomes understanding rather than resolute. He may drink beer, but it will be something European or micro-brewed, not a brand advertised on TV. And if he drinks in public, it will be in the kind of bar his mother would approve. A softer man will receive and repeat new ideas, but he rarely creates them, and rarely fights for them. He likes the great outdoors but hesitates to enter a national park lest he contribute to erosion. He knows the eco-saying, "If you really love Yosemite, don't visit" and thinks it just might be correct.

The softer man is not quite at home with his masculinity. He has heard the feminist critique of traditional, patriarchal men and thinks more than a few charges are true. He hesitates to exercise authority. He would never shout, "I am the head of this home." Instead, he participates in a consensual decision-making process in a house where the question "Who is in charge here?" gets a complicated answer. The softer man certainly is not a tough guy, but he might not exactly be soft either. Rather, he sees the flaws in the tough guy and in the good provider personas and gropes his way toward something better. When an earnest woman tells him, "John, you need to learn how to cry," he wonders if he should gag or take her advice. The softer man is more open but needs more approval. He is less predictable but has a harder time making decisions.

Like it or not, no man born after 1950 can be entirely free of softer man sensibilities. We have breathed the air of feminism, antiauthor-itarianism, eco-awareness, and emotional expressivism. Society has questioned every traditional concept of masculinity, and we cannot help but investigate.

As much as the traditional man in us might resist, the softer man has his good points. First, concerning diapers, the Bible assumes that fathers will be co-parents, if only because work and family time were so intertwined until a couple of centuries ago. The children of farm-ers, herders, and artisans worked alongside their fathers in their homes or on their land. The Industrial Revolution and job special-ization separated what had been joined.

Second, as for expressing emotion and feeling pain, a survey of the biblical data generally yields astonishing results. There are nearly 200 instances of people weeping and shedding tears in the Scriptures, and most of the criers were men. Sometimes the tears were shallow, as people pitied the losses they suffered because of sin or folly. Women like Ruth and Hannah also wept openly. But most often men wept, and for good reasons. Jacob wept over Joseph's reported death (Gen. 37). Later Joseph wept for joy when reunited with his family (Gen. 42—43, 45). David and Jonathan wept when they parted (1 Sam. 20), as did the Ephesian elders when they said good-bye to Paul (Acts 20). David wept again at the death of Saul and Jonathan (1 Sam. 31—2 Sam. 1) and at the critical illness and death of two sons (2 Sam. 12, 18—19). Godly Josiah wept when he read the Law and saw the extent of Israel's sin (2 Kings 22). Hezekiah wept when Assyrian invaders blasphemed God and threatened to capture Jerusalem (Isa. 38). Though they both lived in king's palaces, Ezra and Nehemiah, along with others, prayed and wept over the misery of God's people after their captivity in Babylon (Ezra 3, 10; Neh. 1).

In the Gospels, Peter wept in repentance after betraying Jesus (Mark 14:66-72; Luke 22:54-62). But above all, Jesus wept. He wept in sorrow for His beloved friend Lazarus (John 11:35). He also wept for the city of Jerusalem that had rejected Him and His way of peace and would reap the consequences (Luke 19:41-44). Jesus told men, "Blessed are those who mourn" (Matt. 5:4). Surely it is better to weep over sin and evildoing than it is to be indifferent. The godly know how to weep over wickedness (Ps. 119:136; Jas. 4:9). Some men can go a decade without crying (I think I cried three times in the 1980s). Does that earn us a badge for manliness? Or does it show how much we let culture, rather than Scripture, define our masculinity?

The softer man's ecological sensitivity is also good. After all, God appointed mankind to care for His earth (Gen. 1:26-30; 2:10-15). The laws of Moses take an interest in the kind treatment of animals and in the preservation of valuable trees and other vegetation, and so should we (Exod. 20:10; Deut. 20:19-20; 22:1-4; cf. Prov. 12:10).

Finally, we must admit that men ought to listen to the feminist critique of hyper-traditional concepts of male leadership. Men have often used their physical strength and social position to oppress and humiliate women. Men have silenced the voices and repressed the gifts of strong women. Men ought to listen to the charge that they have abused their leadership position by their selfishness.

Thus, as with the tough guy and the good provider, we can commend as well as critique the softer man. Nonetheless, the softer man seems confused. He is alienated from his maleness, apologetic for his gender. He is so sensitive to criticism of the errors of traditional males that his capacity to lead, to decide, and to exercise strength for others is nearly lost.

THE SELF-ACTUALIZED MAN

Two authors capture the spirit of the self-actualized man, who is becoming the dominant model of masculinity today. In *Habits of the Heart*, Robert Bellah interviewed a number of Americans and found that they live for their pursuit of happiness and purpose in life. They agree that people should pursue whatever they find rewarding, as long as they do not interfere with others' pursuit of *their* purposes. Some individuals find their purpose in self-reliance and hard work, while others find it in relationships; but the freedom to change and grow is essential. Self-actualized men value the freedom to do as they choose, to do their best, and to fashion a life where they have power over their destiny.[3] They want to construct a noble identity.

With their talk of freedom and autonomy, self-actualized men disclose their individualism. They believe in a kind of democracy, but one where individual good trumps the common good. They live in "lifestyle enclaves" where people share patterns of behavior, appearance, and leisure, rather than in true communities. They also believe in a meritocracy. As David Brooks has shown, meritocrats locate their self-constructed identity in their accomplishments, not in their lineage—in their college town, not their hometown.[4] Their merit should bring them a measure of material comfort, they think. But the successful do not go through life hungering for money. Rather, they get a good education and work hard, and then money finds them. Their individualism and meritocratic tendencies make them question authority, but their skill puts them in authority. They attain worldly success but seek inner virtue. Therefore, they will forgo earnings (as long as they are comfortable) to live a richer life. The self-actualized man defines himself by his post, but the post should leave time for sports and leisure.

As before, the self-actualized model of masculinity has positive points. First, self-actualizers see that there is more to life than material success. Second, if self-actualization means developing our gifts and fulfilling our God-given potential, who can object? It is good to work hard and achieve proper goals. We are all made in the image of God, who has goals for all creation and particular goals for His people. God ordained Moses, and no other, to lead Israel out of Egypt. He commissioned Joshua to lead the conquest of Canaan. He called Solomon, not David, to build His temple. In the early church, God sent Peter to the Jews, and Paul to the Gentiles (Gal. 2:7-9). Later Paul told Timothy to learn from "my teaching, my way of life, my *purpose*" (2 Tim. 3:10). The idea of spiritual gifts shows that God has specific purposes for people to this day. Furthermore, the notion that God created, structured, and now governs all things gives "a degree of confidence in the reliability and predictability of life in this world" that encourages the pursuit of goals.[5] Indeed, though God exists outside history, His acts in human history are goal-driven. The goal of redemption drives His relations to mankind, from the fall of Adam to the death and resurrection of Christ. Since God is purposeful and since He created us in His image, we rightly pursue goals.

The problem, therefore, is not goals and achievement per se, but the tendency to choose goals and self-actualizing activities without a moral compass. Self-actualization that has no room for God leads to lawlessness. Men want to shuck off any burden that impedes their self-actualization. They feel free to violate promises and cast off duties they no longer accept. They have no ethical basis, no criteria, to judge one goal or way of life as superior to another. If personal growth or satisfaction are the highest goods, then men will pursue whatever promises that result. Personal gain replaces duty, and "self-expression unseats authority."[6] Men do what they please. Some shout, "No one can tell me what to do." Others, sounding gentler, say, "I need to be true to myself." Sentimentalists say, "I have to follow my heart wherever it leads." But the result is the same. Self-actualizing becomes self-indulgence and ordinary selfishness.

A GODLY MAN

We can recognize our culture's defective ideas about masculinity, but we cannot escape them. Or if we do detect a mistake, we often react and commit the opposite error. For example, feminists reacted to those who accent male-female differences by ascribing all variation, except biology, to cultural influences. Discounting the differences between the sexes, they tried to feminize men and to masculinize women. But a counter-feminist reaction led to a reassertion of male and female uniqueness. Now books like *Men Are from Mars, Women Are from Venus* imply, only semi-ironically, that men and women are not just different species—they come from different planets.

We have examined four models of masculinity: the tough guy, the good provider, the softer man, and the self-actualized man. In describing the strengths and weaknesses of each, I hoped to avoid simply denouncing errors and reacting to them. Please understand:

if we respond to an error by racing to its opposite, the error is still setting the agenda. (If your father beat you mercilessly and you vowed never to lay a finger on your children, even in an appropriate way, your father is still dictating the agenda for your parenting.) So we need to do more than label errors and oppose them. Gathering the good bits from each model will not suffice either.

Instead, we seek a model that gives us the best chance to start afresh. We should neither baptize our culture by sprinkling a few Bible verses on an essentially secular model, nor react to everything that comes from it. After all, no culture can thrive if they discard all of God's ways. I propose God Himself as the model for godly masculinity. Perhaps you noticed the steps we have already taken in this direction:

- In His death on the cross, Jesus exemplified toughness and self-denial for the sake of others.
- In creating the world and redeeming His people, God is the supreme provider.
- Like the softer man, Jesus knew how to cry.
- Like the self-actualized man, Jesus knew what He wanted to do with His life.

That theme will guide us throughout this book. God's saving grace is the foundation for godly manhood. Then, as the man after God's heart seeks a pattern for life, we turn our attention to God Himself. God's person and work will be our model in marriage, fatherhood, work, leadership, and friendship. For example, Christian studies of friendship typically begin with David and Jonathan and Ruth and Naomi, before moving on to friendship in the book of Proverbs. But we will observe that God's friendships are marked by self-disclosure and helpful presence. As for work, the godly man knows and follows God's pattern of work and rest. The chapter on fatherhood does not list techniques for discipleship and discipline; rather, it searches for the essential traits of our fatherly God—justice, love, and faithfulness—and applies them to fathers today. So the man after God's heart lives by grace, not laws; by character, not techniques; in short, by the pattern of the living God.

DISCUSSION QUESTIONS

1. Among contemporary images of manhood, which comes closest to your tradition: the tough guy, the good provider, the softer man, or the self-actualizer?
2. If you asked those who know you best, which view would they say you live by? Which one seems most attractive to you? To most men in your community? Why?
3. Why do so many men sport the tough guy persona? Are tears a sign of strength or weakness? Who cries more—the immature man or the mature man? Explain your answer.
4. How does the biblical image of manhood correct your view and prevailing views today?

PART 2

THE MAN OF GOD AT HOME

3

A MAN AND HIS MARRIAGE: COMPANIONSHIP

From 1985 to 1991, a group of Americans became hostages in a civil war in Lebanon, and their experience illustrates our need for companionship. The hostages fashioned a community in extreme adversity. They lived in stuffy, windowless cells, often scarcely bigger than a grave. Ceilings were so low, they could not stand upright. They endured searing heat in the summer, bitter cold in the winter. They battled mosquitoes and vermin. They wore the same clothes year after year. Filthy blindfolds infected their eyes. Shackled in steel chains nearly twenty-four hours a day, they had ten minutes a day to visit their "toilet," a fetid hole in the ground. They went months without a bath and spent long periods in shuttered rooms without light. Frequently isolated, they were also at times forbidden to speak when together.

Despite the adversity, they forged a community. When permitted to speak, Terry Sutherland taught French and animal husbandry. Terry Anderson made a chess set, a deck of cards, and crude versions of Scrabble and Monopoly from scraps of paper and tin foil and played with competitive zeal. They played Twenty Questions and conducted verbal tours of the world's cities.

At their release, one reporter asked, "In your years of captivity, what was the worst day?" There were several candidates. Perhaps it was the days of mockery when guards surrounded, blindfolded, and chained them, then tossed off mock salutes and shouted "Heil Hitler!" Perhaps it was a day of degradation. One captive was prone to dizziness; so they spun him around, let him go, and howled in laughter as he flailed on the ground. Or perhaps the days of beatings were the worst. Or the days when they prepared for their release, only to see their hopes dashed. Or the days when they were moved like corpses, immobile, wrapped in tape from head to foot and hidden in blazing hot compartments in trucks.

No, they said, the worst day was Christmas. On Christmas they felt their loneliness and the separation from their families most acutely. And the worst Christmas day occurred in 1986. Guards chained together four hostages—Anderson, Sutherland, John McCarthy, and Brian Keenan. They had no books, magazines, or radio. Talking was prohibited, though each was within eyeshot of one of his mates. They knew primitive sign language for the alphabet and used it to communicate, one letter at a time, up and down the chain. But then Anderson took off his glasses, and they slipped and broke, severing the chain. *That*, they said, was the worst day.

That was the worst day because God designed mankind to flourish in relationships. And marriage and family are the primary avenues for companionship. But God also made us so we would seek companions in dorm rooms, work teams, athletic teams, and civic clubs, at church, at home, even in prison.

The story of that miserable Christmas moves us because we are social creatures. We feel those men's anguish because a relational God created us in His image. God is sociable, and when He made us in His likeness, He created us with a yearning to connect with other people. To be whole, we need companionship.

God designed marriage to be the prime source of companionship for adults. Jesus said that God Himself joins men and women in marriage, and what He joins, no one should separate (Matt. 19:4-6). The companionship of marriage is exclusive and intimate, even passionate. But the passion of marriage leads to children, and they create a new kind of relationship. Marriage is a partnership between equals, but parenthood joins unequals. Beyond marriage and parenting is society and all the broad, loose forms of companionship.

All relationships teach us about ourselves, and all hint at the character of our relational God. In parenting, for example, we learn about God's sacrificial love and fatherly care. Children are a bundle of needs; through them we learn the God-like joy of giving—giving to those who cannot reciprocate. In our sweet sacrifices for them, we participate in God's glad mercy toward His children. We taste His compassion for us when we have compassion on children as they cry over some of the silliest but also some of the heaviest things. But nothing matches the most intimate relationship, marriage, for what it can teach us about God and ourselves.

MARRIAGE AT CREATION—SIDE BY SIDE (GENESIS 1)

From the beginning, God designed Adam and Eve, the first husband and wife, to relate in two ways: *face to face* and *side by side*. Face to face, each encounters the other in body and soul. Side by side, they encounter the world. Side by side—or perhaps we can call it shoulder to shoulder—they work to subdue the earth. They rule its animals, cultivate its plants, and develop its riches (Gen. 1:26-29; 2:8-12, 15). In Genesis 1, the emphasis falls on the side-by-side facet of Adam and Eve's relationship. God blesses the *work* of mankind, saying, "Fill the earth and subdue it. Rule over the fish of the sea and the birds of the air and every living creature that moves on the ground" (1:28). Adam and Eve reflect God's image by working. God, the King, rules all things, but mankind rules the world for God, as His vice-regents. Male and female serve together, side by side, partners in governing the good earth.

Genesis 2:20 calls Eve Adam's "suitable helper" for the task, and that has stirred quite a debate about the way men and women work together. *Chauvinists* claim, "See, this proves that women exist to help men!" *Feminists* reply, "No, it shows that men need help!"

But the point is simpler and happier than the debates of gender warriors would suggest. By calling woman a "helper," God does not imply her inferiority. Remember, God often calls Himself Israel's "helper" (Exod. 18:4; Deut. 33:29; Ps. 10:14; 118:7; etc.). Helping does not imply inferiority, for the stronger we are, the more we can help others. I can help my children with their math or science if I know more than they do. But when they know as much as I, my capacity to help diminishes. And if I know less than they do, I can hardly assist them. So, to correct chauvinists, we say, "God designed women to help, but *you have to be strong to help*." Then, to correct feminists, we say, "God designed women to help, so you should be *willing* to help."

The task of governing the earth for the Lord receives the emphasis in Genesis 1. Men and women form a team, offering each other strong and willing help in a grand task. This is the "side by side" of marriage. The "face to face" takes center stage in Genesis 2.

MARRIAGE AT CREATION—FACE TO FACE (GENESIS 2)

Genesis 2 retells the story of creation from a new perspective, using a slightly different sequence. In Genesis 2, God's forming Adam is described in verse 7: "The LORD God formed the man from the dust of the ground." But he made Eve some time later, as verses 21-22 say: "The LORD God made a woman from the rib." Thus Adam and Eve were not a married couple from the beginning of mankind. This gap between the creation of Adam and that of Eve reveals vital principles regarding men, women, and marriage.

Adam's Bachelor Life

God gave Adam the bachelor a series of tasks. The Lord charged him to work the garden, to care for it, to guard it (2:15). The mention of gold, onyx, aromatic resin, and rivers in other parts of the world (2:10-14) hints that the task would eventually expand beyond the garden's borders. Yet as splendid as the earth was, something was amiss (Gen. 2:18). In Genesis 2:15-17, we read that Adam was commanded not to eat from the tree of the knowledge of good and evil. Then 2:18-22 continues:

The LORD God said, "It is not good for the man to be alone. I will make a helper suitable for him." Now the LORD God had formed out of the ground all the beasts of the field and all the birds of the air. He brought them to the man to see what he would name them; and whatever the man called each living creature, that was its name. So the man gave names to all the livestock, the birds of the air and all the beasts of the field. But for Adam no suitable helper was found. So the LORD God caused the man to fall into a deep sleep; and while he was sleeping, he took one of the man's ribs and closed up the place with flesh.

In Genesis 1, we recall, a refrain ended the summary of each day's accomplishments: "And God saw that it was good." That phrase or its equivalent recurs six times (1:4, 10, 12, 18, 21, 31). But now we read, "It is *not good* for the man to be alone" (2:18, emphasis added). This unexpected negative jolts and puzzles us. God detects something wrong in paradise, even though sin has not entered it. Immediately, God proposes a remedy for Adam's problem: "I will make a helper suitable for him." But He does not do so immediately. Instead God appears to ignore Adam's problem and sets him to the task of naming the animals. We are baffled, and God is displeased, but there is no sense that *Adam* is troubled—not yet. But the naming will give us a link.

Naming is an aspect of Adam's *dominion* over creation. Just as discoverers name stars, comets, and diseases today, so rulers named things in the days of old (cf. Dan. 1:6-7). Certainly the naming of the animals required Adam to observe and ponder, "What is this beast? What is its essence? What is a telling name for it?" The verses describing the process are repetitive. God brought the animals to Adam "to see what he would *name* them; and whatever the man *called* [one], that was its *name*. So the man gave *names* . . ." (vv. 19-20, emphasis added). The task, the repetition implies, took quite some time. Then suddenly Adam's singleness, his lack of a helper, reappears. "But as for Adam no suitable helper was found." Why does Genesis return to the problem of loneliness now?

As Adam named the animals, he couldn't help but notice that all had companions, all had mates, except for him! All came in pairs, but where was *his* partner? He surely marveled at God's creatures, but he must also have noticed that none was a suitable companion for him. Dogs make the point. It's fun to romp with a dog, to play rough, to throw a Frisbee it catches midair. And it's relaxing to pat a contented dog that snoozes beside our reading chair. Dogs give almost unconditional love, and some even work hard. But dogs are limited creatures. If we want to frolic, fine; but if we want to discuss life's joys or sorrows, they fail us. We can relate to dogs at their level, but they cannot rise to ours. Only people can discuss matters of the heart.

I believe Adam saw this as he named the animals. God had Adam name all the animals *so he would see his aloneness as loneliness.* Work and animals would never fulfill Adam. He needed more, and he knew it. So God returns to Adam's solitude in 2:20.

The Cure for Adam's Loneliness

However long it lasted, the parade of animals impressed Adam with both his superiority and his solitude. The more he watched the animals, the clearer it became that he had no companion among them. Adam was looking but not finding.[1] Now that the man sees the situation God's way, God creates a woman for him, for Adam is now a man who is ready for her. In his paraphrase of Genesis 2 Ray Ortlund captures the meaning perfectly:

> As the last of the beasts plods off with its new name, the man turns away with a trace of perplexity in his eyes. God says, "Son, I want you to lie down. Now close your eyes and sleep." The man falls into a deep slumber. The Creator goes to work, opening the man's side, removing a rib, closing the wound, and building the woman. There she stands, perfectly gorgeous and uniquely suited to the man's need. The Lord says to her, "Daughter, I want you to go stand over there. I'll come for you in a moment . . ." Then God touches the man and says, "Wake

*up now, son. I have one last creature for you to name." And he
leads Eve out to Adam."*[2]

When Adam meets Eve, he utters humanity's first recorded
words. He does not whistle, *"Vive la difference."* Nor does he moan,
"Here comes the old ball and chain." He breaks into poetry. "At
last!" he cries. "At last!"—after his fruitless searching—"This is now
bone of my bones and flesh of my flesh" (2:23). Here stood the companion for whom he had learned to yearn. She will be his partner.
She is not a threat due to her equality, nor a menace due to her dif-
ferentness. Rather, he thrills at her capacity to fill his longing for
companionship and communion. The woman, his bride and wife, is
a helper suitable for a man because she is of his flesh, yet other than
his flesh. For this reason, he rejoices at her sight and marries her. She
completes him.

It is all too easy for married couples to lose sight of this face-to-
face dimension of marriage. As the years roll by, as children and
career and worthy causes press upon us, even a good marriage can
devolve into little more than co-laboring with a nice person of the
opposite sex who shares our bed and kitchen. The relationship
becomes ever more side-by-side, and the face-to-face recedes.

Even people who teach about marriage can forget this. One year
my wife suffered an intestinal infection by the Giardia microorgan-
ism. On February 1 she got what seemed like an ordinary but severe
stomach virus. Strangely, she got better, then worse, then better, then
worse again over five or six days. Her doctor judged it inconse-
quential, then left town for several days. The symptoms persisted,
and when he returned, we took her in again; but key test results were
delayed. We were still awaiting the results on day 12, but when my
wife got up, threw up, and sank back into bed, I decided to take her
to the hospital at once, with or without the test results.

That process took all morning, and when I got back home, I tack-
led the dirty dishes and laundry that had been moldering for days.
The illness came during my second semester of seminary teaching,
and my reward for a successful first term was an academic overload

in the second. Beyond the extra classes, I also had to deliver a special lecture that week. During those same days, our freezer broke, the children and I got colds, and electrical problems erupted throughout our house. As a result, I was unable to return to the hospital that night or even the next day as I cared for children, house, and work. The next day my wife, much improved, called and asked when I would be coming in. I was just beginning to get organized, and something in me wanted to stay at home and get more work done. But this was the fourteenth day of an illness that began February 1 . . . it was Valentine's Day! I *had* to visit her in the hospital.

On the way to her room, I stopped by the hospital's flower shop. It was only 11:00, but all the classy arrangements were gone. So I went for *big* and grabbed the largest and most expensive bouquet in the refrigerator, something with an abundance of huge yellow blooms. I was just steps away from her door, when—feeling my presence?—she peeked around it. Our eyes met, and we embraced in the doorway. She drank in the flowers and, moist-eyed, whispered, "These are the most beautiful flowers I have ever seen." That was not really so, but I knew what she meant.

We had to cancel the grand date we had earlier planned for that evening. (When children are small, the probability of fulfilling romantic plans for Valentine's Day is inversely proportional to the effort invested in those plans.) Yet we have never had a sweeter Valentine's date than we did that morning, sitting in the hospital hallway for two hours, sipping Sprites, holding hands, and watching the people go by. Why? My wife is "bone of my bones and flesh of my flesh," and during the weeks of her illness and the hectic weeks before it, I had lost sight of that fact.

THE IDEAL FOR MARRIAGE (GENESIS 2:24-25)

During the career-building, child-rearing years, men are prone to forget the face-to-face element of marriage. It helps to return to Genesis 2 and see Adam and Eve thrill at their companionship, at the excellence each saw in the other. Let Adam's delight in discovering his wife be your standard. Yes, marriage thrives on order as well as delight. The last lines of Genesis 2 state the elements essential to good order in marriage: "For this reason a man will leave his father and mother and be united to his wife, and they will become one flesh. The man and his wife were both naked, and they felt no shame" (vv. 24-25).

Genesis 2:24 lists three equal points that together make a strong foundation for marriage. If firm, they are as sturdy as a three-legged stool; but if one leg fails, the relationship will surely collapse. We need all three elements of this trio to develop a healthy marriage.

Leave

"A man will leave his father and mother" shows that the bond between husband and wife trumps the bond between parent and child. It marks marriage as the foundational institution. Some may wonder why God led Moses to specify that the *husband* must leave his family but says nothing about the wife. The answer is that in the culture of Moses' day everyone assumed that the wife left her family. No one had to say it. But Moses adds that the husband must leave too. He must not take his wife into his father's house and place her under his authority. He must start a new family.

Wedding ceremonies wisely embody this in the moment we call the giving of the bride. The father takes his daughter's hand and gives it to the groom, not (originally) to create a photo opportunity, but to show that his daughter is leaving his household and authority and entering another's.

Be United

"A man will . . . be united to his wife" means the husband and wife build intimacy into their new family. They "cleave," as the *King James Version* puts it, meaning they stick close together. They are "glued together," as Paul affirms, quoting Genesis 2 in Ephesians 5:31. They become companions for life, growing in affection and fidelity. They work at their relationship despite its trials and vicissitudes.

Once, after I had spoken on marriage, a young mother of three small children approached me. With her husband just a few feet away, she said, "You know, Bob and I are coming off a pretty bad year. His business was demanding, the kids were difficult, and we clashed frequently. Sometimes . . ." She paused. "Sometimes we didn't even *like* each other. But it's starting to get better."

This woman, this couple, was onto something. When their marriage was unhappy, they knew better than to give up. They were pursuing what the old wedding vows called "troth," as in "I pledge you my troth." Troth is cleaving. Troth is staying power. Troth is a pledge of lifelong fidelity.[3] It is reliability, stability, trust, loyalty, endurance, without preconditions. Prenuptial agreements that set the terms for the dissolution of a marriage before it starts are the antithesis of troth.

Troth is essential to marriage. Its pledge of lifelong fidelity logically precedes sexual intercourse, for it supplies the context for intimacy, for the vulnerability, self-disclosure, and abandonment of intercourse. Troth also permits men and women to bring children into the world without fear that the spouse will abandon them.

Our individualistic culture resists troth. For some, marriage is an arrangement that people enter to gain benefits such as affection, legitimate progeny, and the house only two incomes can buy. But too often divorce is thinkable whenever the costs of marriage outweigh its benefits for a prolonged period. Others repudiate the culture of divorce and broken commitments; but their "solution" is a decision to avoid *all* commitments. They shun marriage. They keep all options open.

The desire to keep options open destroys marital stability. People need a security that unlimited choosing annuls. We must do more than make loving *decisions*. We must make *commitments* and stick with them in ways that cut off other decisions.

Suppose you are in a business meeting when a colleague, David, informs your coworker, Joe, that an attractive young coworker named Jennifer is "interested" in him, even though he is married. Suppose further that David offers Joe his cabin for a tryst. Joe thinks a while, then declines the offer, saying, "Jennifer is attractive, and the offer of the cabin is generous, but I think it would be best for my career and my marriage if I avoided entanglements with secretaries from work." Now think: Would Joe's wife be pleased if she overheard this conversation?

Not at all. Joe's wife does not want him even to *consider* the offer. Wives want the language of fidelity, not calculation. They do not want husbands to ponder the question and decide what is best. They want unshakable resolve, not deliberations. They want their husband to shout, "No way! I'm married."

Without the pledge of fidelity, marriage is merely a wager *for* the persistence of feelings and a wager *against* the ravages of time, illness, and the tensions caused when one spouse achieves more than the other and brings more "benefits." But the man after God's heart does not wager. He loves as God loves—graciously, permanently. If the thought creeps in that his marriage is not turning out to be a very good "deal," if he thinks he could do better on the open market, he remembers that he is remade in the image of Christ—and Jesus hardly got a good "deal" when He took the church as His bride. God is our model, and He told Israel, "I gave you my solemn oath and entered into a covenant with you . . . and you became mine" (Ezek. 16:8b). He kept that oath, though the contribution Israel made to their relationship hardly matched His.

God's covenant faithfulness is our measure, our norm. The faithful love of Christ models the Christian man's marriage covenant. Jesus does not love the church *because* it is pure and spotless—He purifies the church *in order to* make it spotless. Just so, godly husbands love their wives *despite* their wives' blemishes, not *until they get* blemishes. Thus we do not size up our wives each week to decide if we will love them a while longer. The idea of ever-fresh decisions, even decisions to stay faithful, is naive.

During a sabbatical at Yale a few years ago, I attended a Ph.D. seminar that took a personal turn one day. An ardent feminist student described the tension she felt between her Catholic faith and her feminism. She declared, "I believe the church is patriarchal and oppressive to women." She went on to repudiate parts of the Bible that squelch women and contain "texts of terror" for them. Then she made a confession. "Every morning I get up and ask myself if I can be both a Christian and a woman." She hesitated and sighed, "And every day I decide I will remain a Christian . . . even though I know it is killing me as a woman."

We can respond to this in several ways. We can grieve the effects of feminism in this woman's life. We can admire the tenacity of her faith. But above all I think this student's position was unstable. Eventually she must either renounce her brand of feminism or renounce Christianity. There is something wrong with a "faith" that daily considers denying that faith. Of course, this applies to marriage too. *There is something wrong with a marital "fidelity" that is always open to the end of fidelity.* If we daily ponder the option of divorce, we will probably use it one day. To remain faithful, we must stop asking, "Shall I endure?"

Both the woman from Yale and "Joe" who vetoed the affair exhibit *decisionism.* Decisionism, so common in America, invites people to reevaluate everything annually, if not daily. Decisionists keep their options open. They want to be free to reconsider almost any past commitment—marriage, career, beliefs, perhaps even sexual orientation. Decisionism leads some into divorce, because decisionists keep that option open. It leads others to shun marriage. They hate divorce, but because they want to keep their options open, they drift from one semipermanent relationship to another.

Scripture calls marriage a *covenant* that a man makes with the partner of his youth (Prov. 2:17). A man who divorces his wife breaks faith with her, for she is the wife of his marriage covenant (Mal. 2:14). One way to keep our covenant during the dry seasons is to think about our covenant of marriage the way God thinks of His covenant of redemption. God's love for us remains the same, however poor the love and obedience we offer Him. God has maximum troth. A man of God will pledge himself to love as God loves, with permanent devotion to his wife.

That said, we need to remember that our sin and weakness

deprive us of the strength we need to keep our vows. (I once vowed I would never get angry again. The idea was noble, but not very practical.) We want to follow God, but too often we cannot follow through. Thus we must turn to the Lord daily for strength to fulfill our pledges and for mercy when we violate those pledges.

Despite our failures, a place for troth remains. We should still pledge to love our wives "till death do us part." Within the security of such a commitment, we discover what it means to "be united."

One Flesh

After "leave" and "be united," we come to the third leg of marriage: "one flesh" (Gen. 2:24). "One flesh" refers to the sexual aspect of marriage. The next line underscores this: "The man and his wife were both naked, and they felt no shame." The sexual aspect of marriage hearkens back to the idea that Adam and Eve were to "be fruitful and increase in number" (Gen. 1:28). Reproduction is central to our sexuality. Yet we notice that this statement about marriage does not mention children. Perhaps it was superfluous for Moses to mention children again in Genesis 2 since they are so prominent in Genesis 1. Still, the silence about children suggests that while they are the normal *result* of marriage, they are not *essential* to marriage. That is, a couple is truly married even if they do not have the blessing of children.

Furthermore, if children are not essential to marriage, but sexual expression is, then God blesses sexuality even apart from procreation. God designed sex for procreation, but physical intimacy also expresses and deepens love, even if children are not in view.

Finally, while the nakedness of Adam and Eve refers to their physical intimacy, it also refers to their spiritual intimacy. In biblical language, nakedness refers to both physical and spiritual exposure (cf. Isa. 47:3; 2 Cor. 5:3; Heb. 4:13). To be exposed without shame is to have nothing to hide (cf. Gen. 3:7-11). Because Adam and Eve knew neither sin nor guile, nothing shameful separated them. The idea of nakedness without shame suggests their perfect trust, ease, and openness.

Today a proper sense of our sinfulness makes spiritual self-disclosure painful and complicated. We have far too much to hide to enjoy it. Yet in a marriage marked by love and troth, we *can* tell the truth about ourselves. We know our beloved will not use the truth against us. We know we will love each other after the truth is revealed.

CONCLUSION

Our yearning for safe self-disclosure reminds us again that when God made us in His image, He made us for companionship, for intimacy. We should have friends, but marriage is the first and deepest source of companionship on the human level. To develop that companionship, we need to foster both the face-to-face and the side-by-side elements of marriage. We need to carve out time to be alone together for walks, dinners, movies, sports, and vacations. Face to face we develop and maintain shared interests. But we also grow closer when we work together. As we govern the world for God, raise a family, and till our gardens, side-by-side affection and respect increase. If we quiet the critical tongue and foster mutual encouragement, unity develops whenever we labor together in kitchen, yard, or community. Shared labor promotes respect as we see each other's skills at work.

Still, our sinfulness complicates companionship both inside and outside of marriage. The captives in Lebanon irritated one another too—one snored, another was proud, a third too assertive. Husbands and wives bother each other. But the God who built us to yearn for companionship will also enable us to overcome both petty irritations and big problems. Living in God's strength and showing God-like fidelity we can overcome the sin that disrupts companionship and can flourish in a shared life.

DISCUSSION QUESTIONS

1. Is your marriage more face-to-face or side-by-side? Why? How can you make more face-to-face time?

2. If you could spend several days alone with your wife, what would it be like? What might you learn?
3. Of the three elements—leaving, being united, and becoming one flesh—which have you done best in your marriage? Why? Which worst? Why?
4. What happens in hard times if we think of marriage with a decisionist mentality? Why is it important to think of marriage as a covenant rather than a decision?

4

A MAN AND HIS MARRIAGE: THE THREE FACES OF LOVE

The field of evolutionary psychology announces both good news and bad news. The good news is that men and women are designed to fall in love. The bad news is that we are not designed to stay there. Indeed, the tendency to fall out of love is so strong, psychologists say, that we should view a golden anniversary the same way we would view a dog walking on two legs. We should not judge whether it was done well but marvel that it was done at all.

We also have good and bad news from the field of statistics. The good news is that the number of divorces in America has leveled off. The bad news is that divorces are down largely because so many people refuse marriage altogether. They simply live together a while, then split up. Meanwhile, the divorce rate for those who do marry still hovers near 50 percent.

The root of the decline of marriage is the loss of a Christian concept of love. People get married for selfish reasons. Whether they want to have children or want someone to care for them, whether they seek a regular sexual partner or a cure for loneliness, egocentricity drives too much courtship and marriage. Whether it shows itself as lustful *eros* or a desire for the benefits of a traditional marriage, self-interest rules; and self-love cannot long sustain a marriage.

Marriages often start as a hot romance and end as a cool arrangement. In idealized romance, the fuse may be long or short, but once it begins to burn, the rest is supposed to be history. In romance we find the most attractive person in the world—or at least the most attractive person available in our pool of potential partners—the most attractive person who is, as we say, "in our league." For a man, attraction may begin with a woman's physical appearance. A woman may take more interest in a man's ability to provide. It is a good sign if he drives a nice car, and better if, at an early age, he has a professional position and his own office. Kindness and sensitivity count too because they suggest he will be a good father, that he will "be there" for a long time.

Men and women both like to spend time with lively, pleasant people who pay attention to them. ("Can you believe it? She thinks I'm fascinating!") The blend of attraction and attention fill us with warm excitement when our beloved is near. We dream of a pleasant and romantic life together.

But after a while the fires of romance—or perhaps it's infatuation—burn low. The virtues of the beloved become familiar, and his or her vices become grating. Whether a Mozart sonata or a popular melody, even the best music becomes wearisome if we listen to it a thousand consecutive days. Similarly, it seems, even a good spouse becomes predictable, even stale. The strengths are so familiar, the weaknesses so noticeable. As the years pass, we all become wrinkled, colorless, and saggy. Then what? If we marry for romantic feelings alone, and those feelings fade, the marriage faces a crisis. Someone may begin to think of leaving. Or the romance degenerates into an arrangement.

In an arrangement, the two parties are two individuals joined in a mutually agreeable and advantageous relationship. Husband and wife are two equal, autonomous, self-actualizing individuals. They negotiate their relationship. Each gives what they wish and gets what they can. No roles are set in advance; so everything has to be negotiated. Husband and wife both bring something to the table and expect to get something back. If each contributes to the other's happiness through income, nurture, domestic skills, or amiability, then each can expect a return.

An arrangement can seem agreeable, but when a marriage deteriorates into an arrangement, infidelity and divorce become ever-present possibilities. Why remain faithful if a spouse fails to stay as attractive or interesting as he or she once was? Why stay married when the arrangement, the deal, becomes unsatisfactory? Whenever the husband or wife thinks the cost of the marriage outweighs the benefits for an extended period, whenever one party determines it feasible to obtain a higher caliber spouse, divorce becomes an option. Some businessmen trade up for a younger wife every decade or so. J. Paul Getty, the oft-divorced oil billionaire, said, "A lasting relationship with a woman is only possible if you are a business failure."

THE ROOT OF OUR DISTRESS

Again, the root of these troubles is the loss of a Christian concept of love. Both the romantic and the arrangement models of marriage can be selfish forms of love. One seeks raw pleasure, the other the subtler pleasures of security or ease. But in each the husband and wife seek what they hope another will do for them. That is, the quest for a romantic marriage and the quest for a good arrangement can both be driven by self-love, and self-love will not sustain a marriage.

A healthy marriage will manifest three faces of love, labeled by the Greek words *agape, philia,* and *eros. Agape* is the selfless, sacrificial, Christlike love that touches stranger, neighbor, enemy, friend, child, and spouse alike. *Philia* is attraction for a special friend whom we admire due to shared interests or skills, due to their humor or intellect, or due to their personality or approach to life. *Eros* is romantic, sensual love, when fingertips and lips pulse at the thought of contact. *Marriage thrives when these three forms of love join together.*

THE FIRST FACE OF LOVE: ROMANTIC LOVE

Romantic love, *eros,* is a passion, a yearning, for another person who is desirable in a powerful and mysterious way. *Eros* makes us want to reach the depths of another person and bring him or her into the world of our deepest self. When physical yearning and spiritual or psychological fascination join together, we experience romantic love. Scripture does not command *eros*—there is no need. Romantic love is natural. Yet God invites husbands and wives to engage in it, and Scripture commends it.[1]

Eros is born of out of a *need* for another person who promises to complete us. The Song of Solomon describes it this way: "O daughters of Jerusalem, I charge you—if you find my lover, what will you tell him? Tell him I am faint with love" (5:8; cf. 2:5). *Eros* loves one particular person, not all people in general. It chooses one who is uniquely appealing and promising. *Eros* finds that in all the world, there is only one person whom it desires. As the beloved woman says, "I am my lover's and my lover is mine" (6:3; cf. 2:16).

The Song of Solomon often describes the admiration that betrothed and newly married people feel. Solomon describes the delight of romantic love in 4:1-7:

> *How beautiful you are, my darling! Oh, how beautiful! Your eyes behind your veil are doves. Your hair is like a flock of goats descending from Mount Gilead [She is blonde]. Your teeth are like a flock of sheep just shorn, coming up from the washing [They are white]. Each has its twin; not one of them is alone [When she smiles, there are no gaps]. Your lips are like a scarlet ribbon [They are thin and red]; your mouth is lovely. . . . Your neck is like the tower of David, built with elegance; on it hang a thousand shields, all of them shields of warriors. Your two breasts are like two fawns, like twin fawns of a gazelle that browse among the lilies [How breasts resemble fawns browsing among lilies is a mystery, but the main idea is clear]. . . . All beautiful you are, my darling; there is no flaw in you.*

Parts of this poem sound strange to us, but we cannot mistake its sentiment. A man in love declares, "In all the world there is one person whom I desire, only one who completes me."

Solomon also praises romantic love in Proverbs 5. But first he warns his son about the seductive adulteress. Her lips "drip honey," but her steps lead to ruin and death (5:3-14). Promiscuity will devour both strength and riches. But Solomon objects to immorality, not to *eros*. His remedy for sexual temptation is not abstinence but the intimacy of marriage. Hear his counsel (Prov. 5:15-19):

> *Drink water from your own cistern, running water from your own well. Should your springs overflow in the streets, your streams of water in the public squares? Let them be yours alone, never to be shared with strangers. May your fountain be blessed, and may you rejoice in the wife of your youth. A loving doe, a graceful deer—may her breasts satisfy you always, may you ever be captivated by her love.*

"Drink from your own cistern" means to quench your appetites with your wife. Keep your sexual powers in the home. Do not waste them, but treasure them, like the water that was so scarce in Israel. Sexual potency is a resource we must guard and channel, never pouring it into public places, never sharing it with strangers (5:16-17). Then our "fountain"—that is, our capacity and desire for children—will be blessed. Love will grow and endure. Like gazelles, we will mate for life (5:18-19). By keeping sex within marriage, we avoid the trap of adultery. We also bring children into a secure environment.

But sex is more than a means for procreation and a control for unbridled sensuality. Solomon says there is a morally permissible love-ecstasy. He tells his son, "May her breasts satisfy you always, may you ever be captivated by her love." The term translated "captivated" ordinarily means "drunk" in Hebrew (*shagah*; cf. Prov. 20:1; Isa. 28:7). Solomon does not advocate literal drunkenness. Rather he means that a man may fall "under the influence" of erotic love for his wife. A husband may forget himself, losing some of his self-control.

God made us with a capacity to forget ourselves and the world when caught up in certain activities. We get "in the zone" in athletic contests. We "lose ourselves" in absorbing books. We immerse ourselves in noble tasks that demand our highest skills. When that happens, awareness of time, of surroundings, even of self diminishes. We have to rouse ourselves to reenter the real world.

Proverbs permits husbands and wives to lose themselves in love in just this way. We can get carried away in romantic love. God is pleased when we enjoy each other in ways that break the boundaries of ordinary life.

Sometimes Christians do not know how to take Solomon's delight in married sexuality. Thomas Aquinas, a medieval theologian, said sexuality is "always evil" because it produces an "excess of pleasure" that keeps the soul from its highest good, which is the contemplation of God.[2] Now Aquinas was a monk, so I have always wondered how he knew that sex and theological contemplation don't lend themselves to multitasking. But I suppose he is right. Many people can do two things at once, but conjugal relations and theological meditations make a poor pair.[3]

The seventeenth-century Puritans had a higher view. They said sexual union can knit husband and wife together emotionally and will strengthen their love for each other. But they struggled to break free of the medieval Christian's fear of passion. Citing Paul's admonition to consecrate everything "by the word of God and prayer" (1 Tim. 3:4-5), they urged couples to pray for several days after their wedding before coming together. They warned against overheated *eros*, even in marriage, and taught men to pray before every physical act, lest God curse their unborn offspring.[4]

If past Christians suffered from undue modesty and reserve about their sexuality, contemporary Christians often go to the opposite extreme. They accept our society's celebration, even obsession, with physical love. A couple of years ago a survey for a women's magazine discovered that married evangelical women have more frequent sex, on average, than "swinging" singles. There is nothing wrong with regular, even frequent sexual relations, but as always there needs to be balance. The way we celebrate sexuality today, I half-expect someone to advertise, "Become a Christian and enjoy sex like never before." The Puritans probably did have a prudish streak, but we should hear their warnings against using sex for nothing but selfish indulgence. It is possible, even in marriage, to use our spouse for our own pleasure, as an object, rather than loving her as a person. Marriage joins two people, not just two bodies.

We have trouble finding the golden mean that rejoices in the gift of sexuality but remembers the sin of sensuality. But Proverbs got it right. It celebrates ecstasy but warns against a reckless loss of self-discipline.

In most western marriages, the problem is not the getting of *eros* but the keeping of it. The *feeling* of love fades. Like funerals, weddings have the power of prompting reflection in the attendees. Sitting through the ceremony, we do not wonder, "Will these people *find* love?" but "Will they *keep* it?" Slouching in the pew, the divorced ponder, "What happened?" And many who are still married wonder if they can rekindle romantic fires that have burned down to cold ashes. Regarding the fading of love, we can learn something from the second face of love, *agape*.

THE SECOND FACE OF LOVE: SELFLESS LOVE

The biblical word for selfless, God-like love is *agape*. *Agape* is the love that causes God to redeem deformed, rebellious sinners who offer Him nothing in return. We see *agape* love in the Good Samaritan, who stopped to save a (presumably) Jewish man who, by the customs of the day, might spit in his face if he knew who was touching him. We see *agape* when Jesus washes His disciples' feet—even the feet of Judas—getting nothing in return but wet, dirty hands.

Agape is nearly the opposite of *eros*. *Agape* flows not from need but from fullness or sufficiency. *Agape* "does not yearn to get what it needs, but empties itself to give what the other needs. . . . *Agape* is neighbor love: it goes out to all people just because they are there."[5] *Agape* is indiscriminate. It goes out to all, regardless of their worth. *Agape* goes to the good and the bad, the beautiful and the ugly, alike. It loves them because they are there. This is *agape*: "God so loved the *world* that he gave his one and only Son" (John 3:16, emphasis added). Again: "God causes his sun to rise on the evil and the good"

(Matt. 5:45). Again: "God demonstrates his own love for us in this: While we were still sinners, Christ died for us" (Rom. 5:8). *Agape* is divine, supernatural love. We can admire it, but it is against our nature to practice it.

Agape so contradicts our egocentric inclinations that we must ask where we can find the motivation, the strength, for such love; it is beyond us. And surely it is not adequate to admire Jesus as He washes feet. We must do the same. But no one can generate this love by himself. Rather, "We love because he first loved us" (1 John 4:19).

Agape and *eros* seem almost antithetical. *Eros* is passionate; *agape* is dispassionate. *Eros* seeks to fulfill its own desires; *agape* fulfills a neighbor's desires. *Eros* begins with self-interest; *agape* begins and ends with the interests of others. Nonetheless, a strong marriage needs both *agape* and *eros*, both Christian and romantic love.

KEEPING LOVE STRONG: *AGAPE* AND *EROS* TOGETHER

Marriages need *eros*. Christian love alone cannot support a fulfilling marriage. Suppose a woman asks her husband, "Do you love me?" Imagine that he answers, "Of course I love you. The Bible says 'Love your neighbor as yourself,' and since we eat and sleep together, I would have to say we are neighbors—indeed, more than neighbors. So, yes, I love you." No self-respecting spouse could tolerate being loved with nothing but neighbor-love. Worse still would be a profession of love that said, "We have been having some rough times lately. I have also realized that you are dull and untalented, but God commands me to love even my enemies, and as unattractive as you are, I certainly don't regard you as my enemy. So, yes, I love you." Within marriage, no one wants to hear, "I love you because God commands it."

A marriage cannot thrive on sacrifice alone; it needs romance. In marriage, we need to feel special, desirable. We need to feel that we are the apple of our lover's eye, the *one* in all the world for her. In marriage, we need to feel that we are loved *because* of who we are, not in spite of who we are. A woman needs to feel beautiful, treasured. A man needs to feel respected, even admired (Eph. 5:33). He longs to hear, "My hero." She longs to hear, "My darling."

Yet *eros* by itself can never sustain a marriage. Romantic love fades. It also becomes selfish. Marriage needs the tenacity, the discipline, the rectitude of selfless, Christlike love. So *agape* and *eros* must join hands if marriage is to endure and deepen. Christian love and romantic love blend when the person we love needs us and we need them, when they fulfill us and we fulfill them. *Agape* and *eros* blend when a woman loves her husband *because* he is tall, dark, and handsome and *even though* he chews his fingers, picks his nose, and has five other disgusting habits. *Agape* strengthens *eros* several ways:

• *Agape enriches eros* with its realism. It sees the flaws in the beloved and loves anyway. It reminds us that our beloved cannot satisfy all our dreams. It helps *eros* love the whole person.

• *Agape stabilizes eros.* Romance is a flower that blooms and falls. It is a ride in the amusement park—thrilling but unsustainable in the long term. Marriage has its delights, but we spend more time with our heads in the washing machine than with our feet in the Jacuzzi.

• *Agape gives endurance* to marriage when romance cools. *Agape* revives love when it flags because small acts of sacrificial kindness make us feel more loved, make us seem more lovable, and make us want to love in return.

• *Agape corrects eros* when it begins to be distorted by selfishness or sensuality. Self-sacrifice keeps us from using our spouse or keeping her for ourselves.

But *eros also empowers agape. Eros* keeps *agape* from becoming cold and dutiful. It keeps marriage from descending into routine, into a mere partnership in life's struggles. Romance gives us secret joy in serving the one we love. We take pleasure in serving the one we admire. We like to give happiness to the one we love. Such sacrifices seem light, not burdensome.

Romance also keeps the mystery in everyday life. The wink, the hug, the squeeze of the hand, the unexpected kiss lighten the tasks of cleaning up, doing dishes, tending yards, or paying bills. Clouds hover overhead when a tortured commute home punctuates a miserable day at work, but small acts of loving affection part those clouds.

THE THIRD FACE OF LOVE IN MARRIAGE: *PHILIA*

The third, and often neglected, face of love is *philia*, the love of friendship and affection. *Philia* can help bridge the gap between *eros* and *agape*. *Philia* is the fondness we feel for a friend. It is the delight we feel in spending time with someone who is lively, interesting, and warm. Obviously, *philia* stands somewhere between *eros* and *agape*.

- The mark of *eros* is the need for *one* other person; the mark of *agape* is the absence of need for another; but the mark of *philia* is the desire, but not the need, for the company of another.
- *Eros* loves one, and *agape* loves all, but *philia* loves a handful of friends.
- God never commands *eros* and always commands *agape*, but he commands *philia* occasionally (for example, in Romans 12:10).

To evaluate the status of *philia* in your marriage, consider: If you were not married to your wife, would she still be your friend? Would you find her interesting? Good company? In the love of friendship we treasure the pleasant traits of our spouse.

May I tell you about my friendship and admiration for my wife? We were friends for nearly a year before we began dating. The first time I went to church with her, I was amazed at the soprano voice rising so pure, so sweet, so strong beside me. I marveled at the strength and range of her voice. Later I came to admire her touch as a piano accompanist. Whether playing piano, typing, or playing Ping-Pong, she has hand-eye coordination I can only envy. She also graces our home with skill in the domestic arts. Though our society holds such skills in low esteem, she carefully inculcates them in our children. Her smile is quick and warm, and her ready laugh shakes her whole body. I could continue, but you get the point. If I were not married to her, I would still want her to be my friend.

It is important for men (and women) to treasure and even list the excellencies of our wives (and husbands) because the longer we live together, the better we know each other's faults. A man I know commemorated his thousandth day of marriage by presenting his wife with a list of *one thousand reasons* why he loved her. When he told his coworkers about it the next day, a candid fellow exclaimed, "A thousand reasons to love my wife? It would be easier to think of a thousand reasons for hating her."

As the years of marriage pass, it sometimes seems that our marriage IQ gets higher and higher. By *marriage IQ* I mean our irritation quotient. We crack our knuckles or forget to put snack food away. It took me fifteen years to learn to hang up my towel properly, but it took my wife sixteen years to remember to slide the driver's seat back when she uses "my" car. I have banged my knee against the dash so many times that I think I have a slight limp. Joking aside, we all offend our spouses too carelessly and take offense too easily.

Few people are genuinely easy to live with. When we first contemplated marriage, we could hardly imagine the daily irritations that can bloom into daily tensions. Many were hidden—not maliciously—as we tried to make the best impression on a person who was also making his or her best impression on us. Just as important, the virtues that attracted us to our spouses often had a converse vice. A sloppy man admired the neatness and organization of his intended, but now her concern for order feels like ceaseless nagging. A financially careless woman admired her fiancé's financial self-discipline, but now he seems impossible stingy.

Here, too, a list may be in order. But it should be a list of *our* vicious virtues, not our spouse's. Start with your own annoying traits, not your wife's. For example, as a man with a Ph.D., I know that people with Ph.D.s are not necessarily the most intelligent, but they *are* analytical and tenacious enough to become experts (usually) on topics so impossibly narrow that very few would ever want to read about them. Sometimes my wife admires these analytical skills, but I analyze *everything*. When driving, I analyze traffic patterns. When watching a movie, I analyze character and plot development. I cannot help but predict who will die in the action movies and who will marry in the romantic comedy, and I am usually right.

Sometimes my family drives me out of the room so they can watch in peace. In short, I can be annoying. This ceaseless analysis is a vicious virtue. Wise men will recall their own vicious virtues and stop pouncing on their wives about theirs.

Irritations, petty and otherwise, do *eros* in. Disappointment that our spouse is not quite the one we dreamt of can spawn complaints and criticisms that escalate into quarrels. Sadly, some of us have minds that excel in finding flaws, eyes that notice the one white thread on the black suit or the tiny black smudge on the white paper. As the cycle of error and criticism continues, hard words can fly. We feel the pangs of shattered expectations. The fear that we have chosen poorly begins to gnaw at us. Here troth, *agape*, and a firm grip on God's grace must rescue us.

LOVE RESTORED

The family is a society of sinners. A Christian marriage is the union of two redeemed sinners, not two angels. I like to ask my students, "What are the two biggest sources of problems in a marriage?" They shoot back their answers: Communication. Money. In-laws. Sex. Children. Time pressures. No, no, no, I reply, until they beg for my answer, which is this: The two biggest sources of trouble in a marriage are *the husband* and *the wife*. They bring enough sin, enough annoyances, to undercut all three facets of marriage.

- *Eros* fades as we get gray, pudgy, and creaky. But apart from the passing of the years, we let ourselves get stale. We try to be interesting in public, but at home we are dullards.
- Men strain *agape* when they presume on their wives. They abuse troth when they let themselves get lazy and boring, thinking, "She has to love me no matter what." *Agape* knows how to love neighbors, but why test your wife by acting like a mere neighbor?
- *Philia* is love of an admired friend, but there is so much to criticize. We subvert *philia* when we mindlessly irritate our spouses but mind every irritation they inflict on us.

Given our propensity for the sins and follies that weaken love, what can we do? Obviously, wise couples try to nurture *eros, agape,* and *philia*. But we cannot keep love strong in marriage just by *deciding* to do so, any more than we can fix a chaotic schedule by declaring, "From now on I'm getting up at 6:00 A.M." We cannot simply *resolve* to stop sinning.

One way to retain love is to understand our failures better. Consider the cycle of irritations that plague so many marriages. Suppose a man frequently desecrates his wife's beautiful kitchen, tracking mud in from the yard and leaving food and dishes strewn about. He judges that a harmless token of his masculinity, but she views it as a sign of his chronic insensitivity. In return, she criticizes him for negligence and constantly nags him to put things away. He replies by condemning her ingratitude and chastising her for forgetting how hard he works.

Cycles of petty offenses, criticisms, and countercriticisms can suck the life from a marriage. We know better. We know what Proverbs says: "A fool gives full vent to his anger. . . . A fool shows his annoyance at once, but a prudent man overlooks an insult" (Prov. 29:11; 12:16). But how can a couple break a chain of negligence and quibbling?

Two Paths to Reduced Tensions

First, *listen to your spouse*. Men, if your wife says your mud and dishes are driving her to distraction, then they are driving her to distraction, even if you think they should not. When we listen, we forego the right to explain ourselves first, to assert our claims last, and to give top priority to our account of things throughout. Courageous listening observes the marriage without blinking, so that we know it as it is, not as we prefer to imagine it. Merciful listening hears troubles in order to render aid, not to criticize.[6]

Second, *remember grace*. A Christian marriage is more than two people trying to carve out a decent life by following a moral code. A third party is involved. If we pray, and even if we do not, the Father pours His love into our hearts to replenish fading affection and troth. Jesus shows us how to love. He modeled *agape*, loving us when we were weak, unattractive, even hateful toward Him. He entreats us to show the same love if our spouse becomes unhelpful, unattractive, even spiteful. *Agape* loves despite unloveliness and covers a multitude of sins.

God's love rebukes men who think their wives are not quite good enough for them. It shames women who think they cannot endure their husband's poor conduct another day. God calls us His beloved bride after all our infidelities. How then can men after God's heart spurn their wives when they fail to measure up to our standards in ways great or small?

It should be easiest to forgive our wives' sins. After all, we love them, we want peace, and we know they are weak, not malicious. But sadly, it can be hardest to forgive those closest to us. Their sins hurt us more, are often repeated, and often occur despite promises to change. Occasionally a woman does something that so enrages her husband, he resolves to stay angry. He replays and exaggerates the offense to keep his wrath simmering for hours, days, even weeks. But then he thinks, *Is this sin really so great it cannot be pardoned? Greater than my sins against God?* Of course, no one can mistreat us more than we have mistreated God. No wife can dishonor us more than we have dishonored God. Therefore, if God forgives us, we must forgive our wives and seek reconciliation instead of poking our wounds and savoring our bitterness.

CHRIST'S LOVE THE STANDARD

The notion of forgiving our wives because God forgives us brings us to a core value. Remember, we do not live by five-step action plans. We follow the character of our Lord as He remakes us in His image. Therefore, godly husbands see Christ's love as their pattern. As Paul said, "Husbands, love your wives, just as Christ loved the church and gave himself up for her" (Eph. 5:25). I urge you to ponder Christ's loving ways with you and to meditate on His exemplary virtues.

Humility. Christ is the head of the church, but He does not exercise His headship for personal benefit. Rather, He humbled Himself in service, even to the point of death on the cross. So too husbands should see their authority as the opportunity to serve, not to be served. Humble husbands refuse to dominate. They lead by consent, not decree. They lead, but they also empower wives to make decisions about schedules, clothing, food, and much more.

Service. When Jesus gathered the disciples for the last supper, no servant stood by to wash their feet. So Jesus knelt down, like a house slave, to do it Himself (John 13). If our leader washes feet like a menial servant, then we should serve too, in tasks as concrete as scrubbing a kitchen floor. Indeed, such actions are vital expressions of love. Even if wives work exclusively in the home, men can help—and still watch their sports. One game's commercials offer enough time to do a load of laundry and straighten several rooms. Servant husbands ensure that their wives can rest on Sunday.

Patience. One can hardly read the Gospels without noticing how many times Jesus predicted His death on the cross and how many times His disciples failed to get it (e.g., Luke 9:22; 17:25; 18:32). Once Jesus said, "Let these words sink into your ears: The Son of Man is going to be betrayed into human hands" (NRSV). Luke immediately adds, "But they did not understand what this meant. It was hidden from them, so that they did not grasp it, and they were afraid to ask him about it" (Luke 9:44-45). Four times over Luke accents their dullness. But Jesus, a model for us husbands, patiently explained it again and again. Even when He rose from the dead, they could hardly believe it—and He patiently explained the Resurrection to them two more times (Luke 24:26, 46). Let us learn from the Savior.

CONCLUSION

Marriages fall apart because people seek romance and romance fades. They fall apart because people craft *quid pro quo* arrangements, and the *quid* outweighs the *pro quo*. Vices loom larger, virtues seem to shrivel, and discontent sets in. When *eros* erodes and *philia* falters, a marriage that exists to meet egocentric desires is imperiled.

But marriages endure when they join all three faces of love. Wise husbands and wives make time for their face-to-face relationship, to keep romance warm. They treasure their spouse's strengths, to bolster *philia*. They remember *agape*, love for the unlovely, for that is how God loves us. *Eros* and *philia* develop almost spontaneously, but *agape* is more deliberate. Its realism—"my wife is not very lovable today, but I love her still"—promotes truth. *Philia* and *eros* supply the pleasures of marriage, but marriages cannot endure without *agape*, the most God-like face of marriage. For all three, we need God's grace to cover our failings and God's power to pour His love into our hearts. Then we can enjoy the stability of *agape*, the warmth of *philia*, and the heat of *eros*.

DISCUSSION QUESTIONS

1. Which facet of love is strongest in your marriage—*agape, philia,* or *eros*?
2. Are you and your wife friends? How do you deal with the problem of high irritability quotients?
3. List at least twenty things you like about your wife (or husband). Was this exercise easy or hard for you? What did you learn from it? Share the list with your spouse, and watch the results.
4. Read Proverbs 5 and the Song of Solomon with your wife. Discuss the concept of intoxication with love ("a morally permissible love-ecstasy"). When was the last time you prayed about your physical relationship, whether in thanksgiving or in petition?
5. Are *agape, eros,* and *philia* joining together to strengthen your marriage?

5

A Man and His Children

In time, every man faces his limitations as a father. We may see a father act with cruelty or foolish leniency and begin to condemn him, only to realize that we have done the same thing. We may catch ourselves imitating our own fathers at their worst, doing the very thing we swore we never would. Or we may suddenly find that a cooperative child has become a turbulent teenager. None of the familiar ways of fathering work now, and we have no idea what to do next.

Or perhaps we are doing nothing wrong. We simply face the magnitude of the parental task and shudder. For some reason when I first held my third child, a thought seized me: "She is in my hands, but not in my control. She is out of the womb, never to return. Now what? We just got our first two children under control, and now we're outnumbered." We have children on loan for twenty years or so, and we wonder, *Do I have what it takes to be a good father?*

Self-doubt is hardly the first thought we have about parenting. As young adults, most of us read a few articles or hear a few talks on parenting and decide we know everything necessary to solve most parenting problems. When we see a child wailing on the floor in a store we think, *If only those parents had read the article I saw in Better Homes and Babies last week, this would not be happening.* Or we witness a baby loudly refusing to eat his supper and reflect, *If I had a tape of last week's sermon, I'd give it to these pitiful people.*

But after we become fathers, nothing looks quite so simple. As

one man said, "When I was young, I had no children and six theories about the proper rearing of children. Now I am older; I have six
children . . . and no theories."

In actuality, no book of theories or rules is thick enough to cover
every riddle that parents face. Let no one deceive you. Seven-step
plans never took anyone through all the challenges of parenthood.
People think about parenting most when they face a problem and
want a remedy. Naturally, friends and teachers want to help; so they
make suggestions, complete with four-step action plans. But if we
view fatherhood as a series of problems and solutions, we miss the
first and most important principle: Successful parenthood depends
on who you are more than on the techniques you know.

But what should a father be like? Some teachers list series of
virtues that godly parents exercise—patience, fairness, mercy, self-
sacrifice, and tenderness. Parents should certainly be patient, fair,
and merciful. But virtue lists can be as daunting as overstuffed rule
books, since they imply that we should *acquire* all these traits. We
don't have to learn an eight-step plan—we just need to become a new
person! How does that happen? By willpower? By an act of resolve?
No. To say, "Be sacrificial" or "Be tender" is a kind of law too, and
there is more to effective parenting than keeping the rules. Yet, we
must say something about character, for a man can master every
method, but without love, he will fail as a father. Conversely, if a
father loves his children, he can commit many minor managerial
mistakes and yet succeed at parenting.

Fortunately, God does not simply say, "Be loving." God is love.
Because He created mankind in His image, we have the capacity to
love (Gen. 1:26-27). Furthermore, God is remaking His children in
His image. By His power, we share His moral character (2 Pet. 1:3-8).
We grow in Christlikeness until we are conformed to His image
(Rom. 8:29). Jesus says, "Be perfect, therefore, as your heavenly
Father is perfect" (Matt. 5:48). That command is both daunting and
hopeful. It is daunting because God is in Heaven, far above us, and
no disciple can attain His perfect virtue. Yet it is hopeful because He
is our "heavenly Father." "Heavenly" reminds us of His distance, but

"Father" suggests His nearness. Perfection is impossible in this life, but sons do resemble their fathers; therefore progress is feasible.

THE CHARACTER OF GOD AND THE CHARACTER OF FATHERS

God is the source and model for every family, every form of "fatherhood" (Eph. 3:14-15).[1] His fatherly care is the archetype for human fathers. Conversely, good fathers teach us something about God, for their goodness reflects God's. For example, David says, "As a father has compassion on his children, so the LORD has compassion on those who fear him; for . . . he remembers that we are dust" (Ps. 103:13-14). The book of Hebrews compares human and divine discipline: ". . . The Lord disciplines those he loves, and he punishes everyone he accepts as a son. . . . God is treating you as sons. For what son is not disciplined by his father?" (12:5-10).

If good fathers share the traits of God the Father, we need to know God's character. Sometimes people explore God's moral qualities one by one, like a string of isolated attributes. But there is a wholeness, a unity, to God's character. God is a person, and each facet of His goodness holds together in His character. In Exodus 34:6-7 God describes that character to Moses:

> "The LORD, the LORD, the compassionate and gracious God, slow to anger, abounding in love and faithfulness, maintaining love to thousands, and forgiving wickedness, rebellion and sin. Yet he does not leave the guilty unpunished."[2]

Love and justice are prominent in this statement. "Love" appears twice. Further, compassion and grace are forms of love. "Does not leave the guilty unpunished" signifies God's justice. Moreover, love and justice meet in God's patience (he is "*slow* to anger") and His mercy (He notices but forgives wickedness).[3]

Theologians debate whether God's love, justice, or holiness is most central in His relations with His rebellious but treasured creation. When children misbehave, parents ask a similar question:

Should we stress the rule they broke (holiness) or the consequences of their actions (justice)? Or should we forgive them and teach them to do better (love)? Exodus 34 gives primacy to God's love; so godly fathers should too. Exodus 34 lists several facets of love, leading us past vague "love talk." As God describes His own character, the key words describe the facets of parental love.

Compassion is the feeling of love. When life goes against our little ones, compassion makes us feel sorrow and sympathy for them. We mourn when they mourn and rejoice when they rejoice; so they know they are not alone in the world. When a child falls hard or cries at the doctor's office, when they moan that they have no friends, compassion makes us tender. We don't berate them for acting like babies. Of course we instill toughness, but we also give them permission to feel pain, and we feel it with them.

Grace is love's delight in bestowing favors on children. Grace assures our children that we delight in them purely, unconditionally. Grace means we care for our children whether they deserve it or not. Grace takes pleasure in showing a child snow or a Christmas tree for the first time. Gracious parents give their children ice cream even if they have been naughty that day. Grace remembers God's undeserved favors and gives more undeserved favors because of love.

Patience is love's capacity to wait. Patience withholds chastisement or correction from wayward and immature children. It checks the temptation to demand too much too soon, to rebuke too freely. My children first tried to set the table when they were four or five. They realized everyone deserved one copy of each utensil, but sometimes they put the knife on the left and the fork and spoon upside down on the right. Patience says, "Good job, honey. You gave everyone a knife, a fork, and a spoon." A few years later they folded laundry. One child insisted that it was impossible to match our avalanche of white socks correctly. Patience works beside her, reducing the pile, so that the differences between the remaining socks were clear. Later the time comes for driving lessons. Teenagers can persuade cars to do things we never thought possible. (How can a car with sixty-five horsepower lay rubber?) Patience remembers that driving is a complicated skill and says, "Let's try again."

Every aspect of God's character teaches fathers how to live, but some are weightier than others.[4] Love is certainly paramount (Matt. 22:37-40). But Jesus also mentioned what He called the "more important matters" of the Law—"justice, mercy and faithfulness" (Matt. 23:23). Micah cites the same trio: "He has showed you, O man, what is good. . . . To act justly and to love mercy and to walk humbly with your God" (Mic. 6:8).[5] Alongside love, the triad justice, mercy, and faithfulness form the core of godly parenthood.

Some view love and justice as opposites, but justice is a form of love. Justice is love's concern to give each child what is due. Parents "act justly" when they perform the duties they owe their sons and daughters. Justice means parents provide food, clothing, and shelter for their children (1 Tim. 5:8; 6:8). This provision includes an education or apprenticeship that prepares each child for a suitable vocation. In the spiritual realm, parents fulfill their duty by instructing their children in Christian faith and living. Just parents establish household rules that promote a wise lifestyle. Our house has several: 1) Always tell the truth. 2) Treat one another with respect. 3) Don't hit your siblings unless they *really* deserve it. Just parents seal their rules with encouragement and discipline. They distinguish between childish errors and rebellion. They try to discover what really happened, so they can acquit the innocent and correct the guilty.

Mercy is the willingness to overlook and forgive sins. Mercy manifests both love and justice. Merciful parents recognize a child's errors, thereby exercising justice. They also forgive them, exercising love. Merciful fathers see their children's sins, grieve over them, and correct their sons and daughters as tenderly as possible. Merciful parents treat children better than they deserve, especially by forgiving their crimes and misdemeanors. But there is more. The Hebrew term for "mercy" in Micah 6:8 is *hesed*. *Hesed* is covenant loyalty and solidarity. Since covenants are usually between a stronger and a weaker party, *hesed* requires the strong to help the weak. Micah does not simply urge us to *be* merciful; he tells us to "love mercy"—that is, to delight in it.

In the film *Schindler's List*, the commander of a Nazi labor camp executed prisoners for both discipline and sport. Oskar Schindler, who saved every Jew he could by buying them from the camp and putting them to work in his factories, spoke to the commander one day. "You think the ability to kill is power. But real power is to do whatever you want with a life—to take it if you wish—but then to forgive. *That* is power. *That* is astonishing." This intrigues the commander. Soon he is practicing before a mirror, saying, "I forgive; you are pardoned." His chance to show mercy comes when a servant fails to remove a stain from his tub. The terrified prisoner cowers, but the Nazi pardons him with a flourish. But as the boy runs off, the commander reconsiders, grabs a gun, and shoots him. The commander found mercy intriguing for a moment, but he did not love it. We must *love* mercy.

Mercy and justice appear to stand in tension. When parents deal with sins and follies, justice urges punishment, whereas mercy urges forgiveness. But in actuality, justice and mercy are complementary. Children are sinful, weak, and ignorant enough to do many things that *could* merit discipline. But justice needs mercy, for justice without mercy descends into severity. Yet mercy also needs justice, for mercy without justice declines into indulgence and sentimentality. Justice and mercy must cooperate.

Faithfulness is staying power. Faithfulness means children need not fear abandonment. They can count on living at home for two decades, ideally with two parents. Faithfulness means reliability and loyalty that spell security for a child. Faithfulness relieves fathers of the need to decide if they will remain as husbands, fathers, and heads of homes. Faithful fathers commit themselves to persevere precisely when perseverance seems most burdensome.[6]

Jesus called faithfulness "a more important matter." Micah agreed when he summoned Israel to "walk humbly with your God." Walking means consistency, and walking humbly means recognizing our inability. Walking humbly with God signifies more than a self-discipline program. Faithfulness means that children can expect their parents to be *almost* the same yesterday, today, and for a long time. Spasms of goodness and flirtations with virtue are vain. Faithful fathers *dependably* manifest God's love, compassion, mercy, and justice. As we saw, we can simplify these traits to two: love and justice.

LOVE, JUSTICE, AND PARENTING STYLES

The best fathers faithfully demonstrate both love and justice with their children. Indeed, we can describe types of fathers by asking if they practice love and justice *together*. Try to locate yourself on this diagram:[7]

		LOVE	
		−	+
JUSTICE	−	Neither love nor justice: *neglectful*	Love without justice: *indulgent*
	+	Justice without love: *dominant*	Love and justice: *godly*

Most homes have at least one dominant parent. *Dominant parents* are high on justice and low on love. They have lofty standards and expectations but offer their children inadequate support as the children try to reach those standards. Dominant parents act as if rules matter more than children. When dominant parents lead a home, law rules. Laws are rigidly enforced but little explained. Dominant parents say things like, "The rules are the rules." "You broke the rules; now you have to face the punishment." "I don't need to explain myself to you. I'm your father [or mother] and you'll do as I say!"

Dominant parents forget that God never intended the Law to be an impersonal force. His law expresses His character. Because God is truthful, we should tell the truth. Because God is love, we love. Dominant fathers forget that God said He gave us His laws *"for your own good"* (Deut. 10:12, emphasis added). And Jesus declared, "The

Sabbath was made *for man*, not man for the Sabbath" (Mark 2:27, emphasis added). That is, we do not simply keep Sabbath laws for the law's sake. The law blesses us.

Dominant parents think, "Conform to the rules—my rules—and you will be accepted and trouble-free. Break the rules, and you will not be accepted—and I hope you can bear your punishment." They mete out harsh punishments for all violations and find it hard to suspend the laws, even if there are excellent reasons to do so.

Children suffer when love and justice fail to connect. Children born to dominant parents often clam up or rebel as teens. They have a poor self-concept due to a lack of unconditional love. They reject their parents' values because they could never truly embrace them.

Neglectful parents are less common in Christian homes. Neglectful parents provide neither just rules nor loving support. They view children as a burden, an interference. Neglectful parents ignore their children. They use child-care freely and make television and video games into surrogate baby-sitters when they are home. They listen poorly, touch rarely, and hardly look their children in the eye, except to rebuke them. They hate to drop their pursuits for the sake of their children.

Divorce, long hours at work, generations of poor parenting practices, and old-fashioned selfishness all contribute to negligent parenting. Whatever the roots, such parents devalue children. Seeing that they are not even worth their parents' time, children of neglectful parents think they have little value as persons. They thus lack motivation and self-discipline. In time they will find people who care about them, but what kind of caring will that be?

Permissive parents show love without justice, direction, or discipline. This kind of parent is warm and supportive but fails to establish and enforce rules in the home. Permissive parents are lenient, perhaps fearing that discipline will lead children to rebel or to dislike them. They want to play the role of older friend more than parent. Permissive fathers are sacrificial, supportive, encouraging, understanding—and indulgent.

Permissive parents raise children who know they are loved, but the children tend to think everyone loves them in the indulgent way their parents do. They disregard social rules, indulge themselves, leave messes for others to clean up, and manipulate people. They typically lack self-discipline. They are the type who park their car in a handicapped space and race into the store thinking, "That law doesn't apply to *me!*"

Godly parents are loving and just, and faithfully so. Godly fathers have the virtues of the dominant and permissive parents but not their vices. They have defined rules and standards, but they also explain them carefully so children can see their value and accept them as their own. Godly parents punish disobedience, but they take special circumstances into account, give clear warnings before discipline, and offer clear explanations afterward.

Godly parents supply the warm support, the touching, the eye contact, and the ear contact that mark loving parents. They distinguish between real needs (food and clothing) and felt needs (the latest *whatever*), but they sometimes indulge innocuous desires. For example, at a certain age children think their parents need to watch everything they do, as in, "Watch, Daddy—I'm kicking the ball" or "Watch, Mommy—I'm jumping off the diving board." Some say that if a tree falls in the woods and no one hears it, there is no sound. Not really. But children certainly think that if they do something and no parent sees it, it did not happen—or at least they won't be held accountable. It's a silly but innocuous game, and godly parents play along, saving their protests for bigger issues.

The spirit of a parent is revealed by his or her response to various test cases. Imagine two with me.

Case 1: Dinner is ending on one of the last beautiful days of the fall. The rule is, "We clean up the supper dishes before we play." But the girls plead, "It will be dark very soon. Can we all go outside and play soccer first, then do the dishes?"

Case 2: A frantic boy tells his parents that he just remembered he has a report due tomorrow. He needs a ride to the library (seven miles away) to get a book immediately. But the evening's schedule is already full.

Consider how dominant and neglectful parents might respond to these situations:

Case	Dominant parent	Neglectful parent
#1 Dinner vs. play	Rules are rules. If you hurry, you will still have ten minutes of light to play.	I don't care when you do the dishes, but I can't play tonight. I'm too busy to play games.
#2 Library trip	You knew you had this assignment. You need to be more responsible. You'll have to suffer the consequences.	Your assignment is *your* problem. I've got my own problems. You have to work this out yourself.

Case	Indulgent parent	Godly parent
#1 Dinner vs. play	Of course you can play. I'll take care of the dishes for you. You just have fun.	Yes, let's play outside together. But when it gets dark, we'll do the dishes together too.
#2 Library trip	You're tired and under lots of pressure lately. Stay here. Tell me what you want me to get for you.	This isn't the first time you forgot an assignment lately. I'll take you, but you'll have to make up for my lost time.

Discipline, too, draws out the contrasts between the four types of parents.

• *Dominant parents are inflexible.* They think, "You broke the rules—now pay the price."

• *Neglectful parents are undiscerning.* They discipline based on trouble caused, not on evils done.

• *Indulgent parents are weak.* They beg their children to be good, to stop making scenes, to stop embarrassing them. Their authority dissolved long ago. The kids rule, and they know it.

• *Godly parents are strong but discerning and flexible.* They understand exceptions but look for patterns of trouble or neglect. They hate to discipline, but even more they hate to see wrongdoing in their children and will act to remove it. Therefore, regarding the library trip, after investigating they may possibly let a child get a low grade to impress on them the need for greater responsibility.

Children need clear, rational, and enforced rules, rules that work. They also need unconditional love, shown by time and affection. Godly parents provide both, and researchers verify the results. Compared to others, the children of loving and just parents are secure and self-controlled, interested in their parents' faith and values, and capable of heeding authorities.

I suppose it is safe to assume that everyone who reads this book wants to be a godly father. But how?

• Godly fathers establish good rules for their families.

• Godly fathers have a plan for dealing with the inevitable violations of those rules.

• Godly fathers strive to inculcate in their sons and daughters a heart for God.

GODLY RULES

A good way to establish good rules is to adapt the Ten Commandments to family life. The first three commands teach us to worship and honor God at home. Naturally, that leads us to read His Word and to pray too. We thus hallow every joy with praise and sanctify every worry with prayer (Jas. 5:13). The fourth command requires that we build worship, rest, and reflection into our harried lives, that we control our schedules instead of letting them control us.

The fifth command, "Honor your father and your mother," is central. Honor means a child will:

- Follow the general rules of family life (e.g., clear your dishes after meals).
- Obey one-time commands and requests promptly (e.g., run upstairs and close the windows before it starts to rain).
- Perform daily tasks every day (e.g., make the bed, practice the piano, do homework).
- Obey without complaint. (But that doesn't mean there can be no discussion: "If you think we erred, say so respectfully and we will discuss it.")

Commands six to ten apply readily. "You shall not murder" not only prohibits the actual taking of someone's life. It also means to treat one another with respect: "Don't hit, torment, or insult your siblings." Jesus' words in Matthew 5:21-22 ("You have heard that it was said to the people long ago, 'Do not murder, and anyone who murders will be subject to judgment.' But I tell you that anyone who is angry with his brother will be subject to judgment") come into play here. The seventh command reminds parents that strong homes rest on strong marriages. "You shall not steal" is both negative and positive: "Honor property rights. Don't even borrow things without asking." "You shall not give false testimony" means "Never lie; and always tell the truth unless it causes *needless* pain" (that means keeping something to ourselves, not lying about it). "You shall not covet" forbids children from envying the possessions, achievements, or attention their siblings get. (By the way, parents make it easier for children to rejoice in others' success if they distribute praise evenly.)

Parents may need a few more principles regarding siblings. For example, older children may not 1) use their physical strength to take things away from brothers or sisters or 2) use their mental ability to defraud younger children. But younger children also may not use their social (or is it antisocial?) skills to provoke others.

Establishing good rules is important, but parents fret more over their enforcement. How can parents act justly when a child violates the principles of justice? How are parents to *discipline*?

THE DISCIPLINE OF CHILDREN

Discipline ranks among the most difficult parental tasks (a proper discussion might take another book). The difficulty lies with the parent as much as with the child. We misinterpret our children's' motives. We have baggage from our own childhood experiences of excessive lenience or harshness. We get angry about petty offenses one day because we are tired and grumpy and ignore major sins the next because we feel mellow. To remind parents of *their* sins, I define discipline this way: "Discipline is the process in which bigger sinners attempt to convince littler sinners to mend their wicked ways."

That is not a full definition since discipline is positive as well as negative. It involves both nurture and admonition, both education and punishment (Eph. 6:4). But the main point stands: Parents cannot consider themselves models of humanity and treat their children as miscreants. We suffer too much from bad patterns and bondage to custom (as well as ordinary sinfulness) to tout ourselves as exemplars of virtue.

Bad Patterns

Most of us have two tapes going in our head. Tape 1 is: "My mother said this, my mother did that." Tape 2 is: "My father said this, my father did that." We tend to accept and imitate the tapes we like, almost blindly, and, just as blindly, to reject and react against others.

For example, I had a tape called "What to do when something spills at the dinner table." To understand my tape you must know that my father's family escaped from Communist Russia in 1935. Growing up in Stalinist Russia, where millions died of starvation, he came to America at the height of the Depression. So my father had zero tolerance for spilled milk or juice when my brothers and I were growing up. Contrary to the second law of physics, our actions led to opposite but unequal reactions. Looking back, I'm sure I exaggerated my innocence, but I remember thinking, at an early age, that my father got too upset about spilled milk. And I vowed, "When I have children, I will never yell at them for spilling anything."

I kept my vow and was pleased with myself. I have lost my self-control more than once, but never for spilling. My children, dimly aware of this, eventually began to knock cups over almost every day. Maybe it looked like a game to them: Topple a cup and watch Mom and Dad jump up and scramble around to sop it up. One day as yet another cascade of milk and orange juice drenched the table and floor, my wife fixed her eyes on me and said, "I'm thankful that you are true to your vow not to yell, but we're losing about a gallon of milk a week. We have to do something!"

She was right, and we did do something. But mark this: Mindless *imitation* of our parents lets them establish the agenda for our parenting, but so does mindless *rejection*. When we react to our parents by reversing whatever they did, they are still setting the agenda. Godly parents liberate themselves from the pattern of imitation and rejection and, with God's guidance, find their own wisdom.

Bondage to Custom

To find our own wisdom, we must also evaluate our culture's customary wisdom, which dominates us more than we realize. It is customary today for parents to use three forms of discipline: spanking, loss of privileges, and banishment from civilized society (a.k.a. grounding). All of these have a place. Proverbs commends the use of the rod—we call it *spanking*—on occasion. Spankings should sting but should never hurt a child physically (therefore lightweight, wooden "spanking spoons" are preferable to the hand, which can be too heavy). All discipline is "painful," says Hebrews 12:11, making it fair to say that if there is no pain of any kind, sinful behavior has not been disciplined. The pain of a spanking teaches a child that sin leads to pain.

Deprivation of privileges sometimes works too. If a young boy and his friend tear up the basement, perhaps that friend should not visit for a while. If an older girl violates a curfew, she may justly lose one night out the next weekend. But other deprivations hardly stand up to reason. For example, some parents deprive children of television (or other electronics) for almost every offense. If their room is a mess, no TV. If they fail to do their homework or fail to take out the garbage, no TV. The punishment is arbitrary and wrongly accentuates one privilege.

Banishment from civilized society also works on occasion. If a boy eats like a caveman, perhaps he should eat alone in his room once. If two siblings bicker all morning, parents may punish them by forbidding them to occupy the same room for a while. But sending children to their room for every offense makes no sense.

Liberation from Custom

Unfortunately this trio of disciplinary methods does not give parents enough room to educate. And sometimes none of them seem to work. My wife once put it this way as she struggled with a child who was going through a period of mild rebellion: "I don't know what to do with her. She's too old to spank. Take away her privileges? She hardly notices the television or radio. All she does is play the piano and play soccer, and they are both so worthwhile. I certainly don't want to ground her—I'd be punishing myself as much her." I said, "Good point. I'll get back to you on that."

Six weeks later (theologians answer questions rather slowly sometimes) I was reading Exodus 21:22-25 and found it addressed the point:

> *If men who are fighting hit a pregnant woman and she gives birth prematurely but there is no serious injury, the offender must be fined whatever the woman's husband demands and the court allows. But if there is serious injury, you are to take life for life, eye for eye, tooth for tooth, hand for hand, foot for foot, burn for burn, wound for wound, bruise for bruise.*

Lest you worry, I had not suddenly developed a vindictive streak. Though it sounds harsh, the purpose of this law is actually to *restrain* vengefulness. It forbids excess, as in, "If you knock out my tooth, my friends and I will knock out all of yours." The law forbids spirals of violence, declaring, "*One* tooth for *one* tooth, nothing more."

The principle of proportional punishment is foundational for the Bible's penal code. It governs property violations (Exod. 22:4-6), personal injury (Lev. 24:19-20), and manslaughter (Lev. 24:17, 21). It is perhaps clearest in the case of perjury, where the convicted perjurer must suffer precisely the punishment that his lie would have inflicted on his victim (Deut. 19:16-21).

In the home, the goal is reform, not punishment per se. Therefore I prefer the phrase, *the principle of proportional discipline*. Proportional discipline is neither too harsh nor too lenient. It is relevant to the misdeed and is measured to suit it. If tooth crimes merit tooth punishment, then food crimes deserve food punishment and clothing crimes merit clothing discipline.

For example, if grade-school children spill juice day after day, proportional parents will warn them, then take juice off their menu for a day or two. When we instituted this in our house, the spills promptly stopped.

Or consider that chronic cause of parental distress—a child's habit of dropping book bags and coats on the floor the instant they enter the house. With a mere shrug of the shoulders, coats and bags slide effortlessly to the floor. Too often parents shout and threaten—and then pick it all up! Instead, try a book bag punishment for a book bag crime:

"Honey, I see that you don't care very much about your book bag since you drop it in the middle of the floor so much. So, unless you stop doing that, we will put it away for a couple of days."

"But how will I get my books and lunch to school?"

"Well, I guess you can take them to school in a grocery bag."

"A *grocery* bag! Are you kidding? Everyone would laugh at me!"

"All right, you have one more chance to hang up your bag. But if you drop it on the floor again tomorrow—that would be the third day in a row—it will go on the shelf for three days."

This works for all sorts of crimes and misdemeanors. Abuse your new coat, lose your new coat (and get an old ugly one from the old clothes box). Abuse the television, lose the television. Fail to do chores on time, get double chores the next day. If two children bicker for a solid hour while playing, they are forbidden to play together for an hour.

Occasionally someone tells me this is cruel. First, let me be clear. Children may go to school without *their* coat, but we never send them, in winter months anyway, without *any* coat. Or children may briefly go without juice, but we never malnourish them. No child ever contracted scurvy by going two days without vitamin C.

Furthermore, I believe it is far more cruel to yell at children and threaten them without doing anything to root out their sin and error. It is far more cruel to teach, by our inaction, that sins have no consequences.

This leads us to the essence of discipline. All parents discipline their children. But if we lose sight of justice, we discipline for the wrong reasons. We discipline them for acts that are troublesome or embarrassing to us, even if they are accidents. But we overlook sin and rebellion if they cause us no trouble. If parents discipline their children for selfish reasons, they destroy its essence. God disciplines us, individually, so that we might live and enjoy His righteousness and peace (Heb. 12:9-11). He disciplines us corporately to purge evil from the land (Deut. 13:5; 17:7). Similarly, parents should seek to free their children from evil. Our thought as we discipline should be, "I love you too much to let you think that what you did has no consequences." Discipline is like a vaccine. It inflicts lesser pain now to avoid greater pain later.

One question remains: Can godly fathers change a child's heart?

A HEART FOR GOD

We have discussed the character, the rules, and the discipline of a godly father. But how can we convey all this to our children? We cannot simply command children to develop character. Fathers cannot control a child's character the way they can control their behavior. The heart of a child is partially hidden. It belongs to the child, and it belongs to God, but not to us. Like the heart of a king, the heart of a child is in God's hands. Only God can quicken that heart, and only the child can respond.

Nevertheless, parents can help inculcate character. By sharing our heart for God, we can mediate God's presence. Proverbs 13:20 observes, "He who walks with the wise grows wise, but a companion of fools suffers harm." As Moses says in Deuteronomy 6:4-8:

> *Hear, O Israel: The LORD our God, the LORD is one. Love the LORD your God with all your heart and with all your soul and with all your strength. These commandments that I give you today are to be upon your hearts. Impress them on your children. Talk about them when you sit at home and when you walk along the road, when you lie down and when you get up. Tie them as symbols on your hands and bind them on your foreheads.*

Notice the sequence. First, parents know, love, and obey God. *Then* they can impress those values and priorities on their children. To develop the spiritual life of their children, parents must first develop their own. Many parents prematurely ask about techniques for spiritual nurture. They want to know *how* to have good family devotions or *when* to talk to their children about the faith. Good questions! But *who* we are matters more than the techniques we master.

Living faith expresses itself naturally whenever we are with our children. So when should we talk about our faith? Breakfast is a good time, for then we can gain a spiritual perspective on the day. Lunch works too because we can evaluate the morning and make midday corrections. Supper is fitting as well because we can review the day and prepare for the evening. Bedtime is sensible also because tired children tend to be spiritually receptive.

Just as all occasions offer opportunities, so do all places. At the store, we can discuss money and the difference between needs and desires. After an athletic contest, we can consider exercise and competition, and also the importance of doing our best and leaving the results to God. Reviewing a television program, we can ask what kinds of humor enrich and what kinds humiliate. After church, we can recount what we learned in worship or Sunday school.

As we share our hearts and minds with our children, they acquire our understanding of God. This has an enormous impact on children. In our home, we don't watch much TV, but we tend to watch together (we have one television) and discuss what we see, including commercials. Likewise, when we listen to popular music, we analyze the lyrics. This paid off one day when two of our children, ten and eight, started playing an old Billy Joel tape they had found. I tuned it out until I heard the upbeat nihilism of the song, "Only the Good Die Young." Hearing my children bouncing to the music downstairs, I knew we had to talk about the lyrics. Descending the steps, I heard one child shout over the music, "That's not true at all!" The other replied, "Yeah. Remember Great-Grandma? She was really good, and she lived to be ninety-eight." Mission accomplished! Indeed, "He who walks with the wise grows wise."

Christian parents nurture their children as they walk and talk together, discussing friendships, school, sports, and social pressures. Some men delude themselves with notions of "quality time" as in, "I don't have much time with my children, but at least it's quality time." But we cannot treat children like business appointments. We cannot appear at their bedroom door on Saturday and say, "It's 9 A.M. Are you ready for our quality time?"

It is nearly impossible to schedule quality time. *Quality* time comes through *quantity* time. Noble plans for quality time often sour. Routine time together supplies the hours we need so golden minutes will emerge. Children need us to be home several nights a week and for entire weekends. Children need fathers more than Dad needs a promotion and more than the kids need trombone lessons. Working together, fathers teach children how to work. Traveling with Dad in the car, they start to learn to drive. Invite a young child to join you on an errand, and he will jump at the chance. Use it.

CONCLUSION

I once went to a baseball game with my middle daughter. We sat in cheaper seats, but as the game ended, we briefly slipped behind home plate. I realized we were in ideal position for a foul ball and mused, "I've been to lots of ball games but have never caught a foul ball. It's a shame we didn't bring a glove because if a ball comes our way, it will have too much speed and spin to catch with our bare hands. Still, we might get one if a ball bounces off someone's hands a row or two ahead of us." Sure enough, seconds later the batter sent a hard foul straight toward us. One row ahead, a man rose for the ball. I prepared for the bounce, but at the last instant he ducked. I threw my hands in front of my face, and, just as I had predicted, the ball spun off my palm and bounced to another fan a few feet away. A tragedy? Not at all. My daughter and I had a great conversation about hopes and disappointments. Quantity time led to quality time.

Fatherhood is glorious but daunting. To show love, justice, and faithfulness is a noble but elusive aspiration. We want to enact wise laws and to practice firm but gentle discipline, but whence comes our strength? Again, "He who walks with the wise grows wise." If we walk with our wise heavenly Father, he will impart wisdom to us to share with our children.

Discussion Questions

1. As a parent, are you oriented more to justice or to mercy? Which of the four parenting types best describes you?
2. If God is truly remaking you in the image of His love, compassion, grace, patience, faithfulness, and justice, as described in Exodus 34:6-7, what does that mean for the way you treat your family?
3. Describe your current patterns for disciplining your children. Restate the principle of proportional discipline in your own words. Where might you practice it in your home or in other relationships?
4. Do you spend enough time walking and talking with your children? How can you spend more time with them?
5. How do the "tapes" of what your father and mother said and did influence you today?

PART 3

THE MAN OF GOD in SOCIETY

6

A Man and His Friends

During the years when men choose a marriage partner, establish a career, start a family, and order their finances, the pressures of life squeeze out the zeal men once had for their friendships. Men need friendships, but for the bulk of their adult life, they are so careless about them, they may not know if they have true friends or not.

The Church—a Friend of Friendship?

Christians believe in relationships; therefore they defend the family and welcome strangers into their midst. Christians will also lament their lack of friendship and critique the way our culture mitigates against it. Yet the church itself is more than a little ambiguous about friendship. Churches gather for "fellowship" and "community" but do not promote gatherings for "friendship." Historically the church has advocated "spiritual direction" where mentors lead novices toward discipleship. But the church seldom mentions the mutual direction that friends offer each other as peers. It is not hard to see why friendship has become the forgotten form of love.

If we compare the love of friendship (*philia*) to love of neighbor (*agape*) as Jesus describes it, we can understand the church's relative indifference.[1]

- *Agape* is indiscriminate, extending itself to every neighbor or stranger; *philia* discriminates, extending itself to those whom it favors.

- *Agape* goes to all who cross its path; *philia* goes to a few who make sure their paths cross.
- *Agape* is inclusive and denies no one; *philia* is exclusive and denies many.
- God's love is the source and model of *agape*; human attraction is the source of *philia*.
- *Agape* is divine, unmerited love; *philia* is a human love based on affection for the desirable.

Some Christian literature about friendship illustrates the difficulty. Em Griffin explains that in the attraction between potential friends, "the thread of increased self-esteem is woven into each principle of attraction." A friend is someone who "makes me feel good about myself."[2] Griffin knows this may leave his Christian readers uneasy. But he lists factors that foster the good feeling between friends: proximity, collaboration, physical attractiveness, competence (but not omnicompetence), affirmation ("we appreciate those who appreciate us"), the exchange of favors, and similarity of skill, background, and interests. The common thread, Griffin concludes, is "our overriding need for self esteem."

> Most of us have some lingering doubts about our attitudes and lifestyle. Having people close who think and feel as we do can be very comforting. The law of selective exposure suggests that we avoid information that challenges our beliefs. Friendship is probably the purest form of selecting our own propaganda. Relationships with similar others make us feel good about who we are.[3]

Not only do friends make people feel good about themselves—they may also make others feel bad, for "to announce, 'You are my friend' to someone, is, by implication, to say to another, 'You are not.'"[4] This exclusivity, even selfishness, makes the church uneasy about friendship.

C. S. Lewis is a friend of friendship but has some caveats. Mutual affirmation and shared insights can, he notes, render friends indifferent to the opinions of others. A self-appointed group of friends easily acquires a superiority complex, becoming a coterie of snobs, proud that they rise so far above others in skill, virtue, or insight. Because shared convictions can galvanize people to take a stand, friendship can empower resistance to authority, for harm as well as good.[5]

Finally, friendship is more transitory than other kinds of love. *Agape* can appeal both to duty and to the love of Christ. With familial love, we have both social and physical motivations to show affection and fidelity. But fewer moral or spiritual resources sustain friendship. So the church neglects mere friendship, except for a few overused remarks on fidelity and honesty.

THE VALUE OF FRIENDSHIP

Despite these weaknesses, the Bible's testimony should motivate us to seek strong friendships. Ecclesiastes 4:9-12 describes the four advantages of friendship. First, friends work together effectively: "Two are better than one, because they have a good return for their work" (v. 9). Second, friends help one another in time of need: "If one falls down, his friend can help him up. But pity the man who falls and has no one to help him up!" (v. 10). Third, friends offer comfort and companionship in life's cold nights: "If two lie down together, they will keep warm. But how can one keep warm alone?" (v. 11). Fourth, friends cushion the blows life deals us: "Though one may be overpowered, two can defend themselves. A cord of three strands is not quickly broken" (v. 12). Friends galvanize us for God-given crusades.

In short, friends *help* each other. Some of us like to give aid but can hardly receive it. It embarrasses us to ask. Or we accept it only if we can reciprocate. If we receive help four times before repaying it, we would rather suffer in silence than receive assistance a fifth time. Friends cut through our pride and say, "You need my help, and you are going to get it whether you like it or not." But perhaps the greatest help a friend gives is himself, his companionship.

Sometimes a Man Needs Another Man

Marriage and family are the principal avenues for companionship. As we saw in Chapter 3, when God created mankind, He fashioned a couple in relationship. Face to face, they expressed their love; side by side they worked to govern God's earth. God created Adam first, and that first man worked the garden alone for a time. But soon God declared, "It is not good for the man to be alone. I will make a helper suitable for him" (2:18). Yet, instead of addressing Adam's loneliness right away, God appointed him to name the animals. As Adam observed and named the animals, he had to see that all had companions except him. As they paraded by, Adam began to see that he needed a partner too. The marriage of Adam and Eve was more than a friendship, but it certainly was not less. So God ordained marriage, in part, to cure loneliness and to provide companionship.

But marriage can never fully satisfy the human longing for companionship. In America nearly 40 percent of all adults over eighteen are single. The number is not much lower in the church. These single people need companionship. Furthermore, despite expectations, many marriages lack deep companionship. And even an ideal marriage cannot fulfill all our needs for companionship. God did not intend one person to supply another person's every social need. To expect a spouse to rejoice at each of her husband's triumphs, to weep at each setback, to converse helpfully upon each topic is folly. That is an impossible standard, and it approaches idolatry. Even married people need a circle of friends.

Besides, even the happiest married man wants to talk to another man about certain things. Suppose a businessman has begun to realize that he works long hours, in part, because he actually likes work more than family and leisure. At work he is an important person. His words, his decisions, change things. People admire him in the workplace; they love to do him favors. But when he gets home, the children always seem to be squabbling, and his wife wears that all-too-familiar "where have you been?" frown. A wise man will disclose his sentiments to his wife, but he might talk to a man who has faced the same problem first.

Sometimes we just need to talk to someone of our own gender. Suppose a woman of unspecified age looks in the mirror and says, "I am getting wrinkled, gray, fat, and ugly." If she tells her husband, he might try to reason her out of it. "You have very few wrinkles and gray hairs for your age, and besides you can dye your hair. And you're not fat, just a little overweight . . ." But a woman does not want a four-point analysis of her physical condition—she wants sympathy. She might get it from a woman who knows the melancholy sensation of watching one's beauty fade. Similarly, a man might think, "I have no friends." If he tells his wife, she might take it personally: "I thought *I* was your friend!" Or she might just feed his self-pity when he really needs someone to talk him out of his funk. It might be best to call an old buddy.

Sometimes a Man Needs a Rebuke

Earlier we saw that friendships can degenerate into mutual admiration societies. But friends also have the capacity to cause *creative discomfort*. Griffin says friends make us feel good about ourselves. Perhaps, but true friends also inflict *constructive misery* on each other. Friends make us feel bad about ourselves if there is good reason for it. Certainly God, the model friend, stings in order to heal.

Friends correct each other, and they listen when the correction comes. Remarks that would seem judgmental from an acquaintance become loving counsel in the mouths of friends. "Iron sharpens iron," and sometimes the sparks fly (Prov. 27:17). As Proverbs also says, "Better is open rebuke than hidden love. Wounds from a friend can be trusted" (27:5-6). And again, "The pleasantness of one's friend springs from his earnest counsel" (27:9).

Once I saw a married friend developing a close relationship with an attractive single woman. A strong-willed man, he was also in a spiritual slump and in no mood to hear a rebuke. If I spoke, I thought he might sever our relationship. But I spoke anyway, because I loved my friend more than I loved our friendship.

Friends have challenged me too. Once my wife and I visited friends who had moved to another state. Carol had allergies somewhat like mine and was eager to share how she got relief by changing her diet. I am skeptical about all-rice diets and such; so I tried to deflect her with lighthearted remarks about oat chaff riding to our rescue. Everyone laughed—except Carol. With flaming eyes and steely voice, she said, "I see what you're doing, Dan. You don't believe a word I'm saying, but you're too polite to say so; so you're making it into a little joke. You don't have to do what I'm saying, but at least listen. It just might help you." I appreciated her honesty and thought, *Wow, what a friend*.

So far we have explored the values and dangers of friendship. Next we will probe Scripture to learn how to preserve the best and avoid the worst of friendship. We need a model of an ideal friendship.

THE GOD-CENTERED MODEL FOR FRIENDSHIP

The Bible makes few statements about friendship, though there are some remarks in Proverbs and Ecclesiastes and illustrations from the lives of David and Jonathan, Ruth and Naomi, Jesus and His disciples.[6] Sadly, many talks on friendship run through a string of verses from Proverbs to generate an atomistic list of human virtues titled "The Traits of a Friend." The format is somewhat legalistic: "A good friend is faithful, righteous, and loving, willing to sacrifice and willing to rebuke. If you want to please God and your friends, seek these traits in your relationships."

But that, of course, returns us to Nike Christianity. We destroy the Gospel when we quote strings of isolated verses from Proverbs and say, "Do this and this. Be that and that." Proverbs does show us the way of wisdom. The problem is, we cannot follow that way in our own strength, as Proverbs itself says (3:7-12). We must ground friendship in something deeper than duty. That something is the nature of God, the archetypal Friend. He shows us how to be a friend, but more, He remakes us in His image (Rom. 8:29; Eph. 4:22-24). As He does this, He grants us the ability to do what Proverbs says. Then we can do for others as He has done for us.

Believers understand intuitively that God is their friend. Though the Bible only calls God a friend five times, we readily see that the central traits of God as friend are *self-disclosure and helpful presence.* These traits manifest themselves first in God's dealings with Abraham, "God's friend" (Jas. 2:23; cf. 2 Chron. 20:7).

In Genesis 18, the angel of the Lord visited Abraham and Sarah when they were ninety-nine and eighty-nine years old. He came to announce that He would *help* them, that Sarah would bear the child He had promised them twenty-five years earlier. The angel shared a meal with them and confronted their doubts. Then, as he prepared to leave, He asked, "Shall I hide from Abraham what I am about to do?" God had chosen Abraham to be the Father of Israel, and now He revealed His plans to judge Sodom and Gomorrah (18:17-21). Thus God *disclosed Himself* to Abraham. He was just and could not tolerate the wickedness of those cities. Abraham found this troubling, and as the Lord turned toward Sodom, the patriarch asked God if He would destroy Sodom if there were fifty or ultimately even ten righteous people in it. While Abraham had concern for Sodom, he was also probing the character of God. "Will you sweep away the righteous with the wicked? . . . Far be it from you to . . . [treat] the righteous and the wicked alike. . . . Will not the Judge of all the earth do right?" (vv. 23-25). Is God just in His judgments? Is He merciful? Yes, for He would spare the whole city of Sodom for the sake of even ten righteous men (v. 32). Thus God revealed His justice and mercy to Abraham, His friend.

The Bible also calls Moses the friend of God, in Exodus 33:7-11. As a friend, God helped Moses lead Israel out of Egypt. Yet, as in Genesis 18, the strongest element of Exodus 33 is God's *self-disclosure.* Shortly after Israel left Egypt, the Lord manifested His presence with Israel in a "tent of meeting" located outside the camp. Many visited the tent, but when Moses went, the glory-cloud of God would descend on it, and the Lord, would "speak to Moses face to face, as a man speaks to his friend" (v. 11). Later the Lord disclosed Himself more fully, letting Moses see the "back" of His glory as He passed by on a mountain (vv. 18-23). He declared His nature to Moses: "The

LORD, the LORD, the compassionate and gracious God, slow to anger, abounding in love and faithfulness, maintaining love to thousands, and forgiving wickedness, rebellion and sin. Yet he does not leave the guilty unpunished" (34:6-7).

The third time the Bible calls God a friend, Isaiah emphasizes His helpful presence. Although Israel had no claim on His friendship, the Lord called Israel and became her friend. Isaiah says:

> But you, O Israel, my servant, Jacob, whom I have chosen, you descendants of Abraham my friend, I took you from the ends of the earth, from its farthest corners I called you. I said, 'You are my servant'; I have chosen you and have not rejected you. So do not fear, for I am with you; do not be dismayed, for I am your God. I will strengthen you and help you; I will uphold you with my righteous right hand.
>
> —41:8-10

Jesus shows the same traits in His friendships: self-disclosure and helpful presence. Like the Father, He befriends the undeserving. His foes accuse, "Here is . . . a friend of tax collectors and sinners" (Matt. 11:19; Luke 7:34). He also calls Himself the friend of His disciples, showing the same two traits. In John 15:13-15 He says, "Greater love has no one than this, that he lay down his life for his friends [helpful presence]. You are my friends if you do what I command. . . . I have called you friends, for everything that I learned from my Father I have made known to you [self-disclosure]."

Of course, God's friendship with Israel does not directly model a *typical* human friendship. Above all, no human friendship could be so one-sided. God knows us perfectly; so we need not disclose ourselves to Him, whereas He chooses to reveal Himself to us. Further, He helps us despite our disloyalty, and we can ultimately give nothing to Him. So self-disclosure and helpful presence take a different form in human friendships.

Beyond help and disclosure, nobler human friendships feature a third thing—a secret, an insight, a cause, or a passion. Two children may become friends because of one of life's small accidents. Perhaps both moved from Oklahoma, or both are brainy nerds and are estranged from their fathers. But usually there is more. As C. S. Lewis says:

> Friendship arises out of mere Companionship when two or more of the companions discover that they have in common some insight or interest or even taste which the others do not share and which, till that moment, each believed to be his own unique treasure (or burden). The typical expression of opening Friendship would be something like, "What? You too? I thought I was the only one."[7]

So human friendship is more than a mutual aid society, more than an exchange of favors. Friends help each other, but, more deeply, they share a secret, an enthusiasm, a cause, not just a task. They have a common insight about how the world is and a common dream about how it ought to be. Their bond surpasses the unity of a team of workers or athletes who hope to accomplish something together, for it encompasses a mutual passion for a principle or a way of life. They have a common ideal for the fulfillment of the work or the playing of the game. And they welcome others who share that ideal.

Once we know the pattern for friendship, we can read Proverbs with less danger of falling into legalism. Proverbs is no checklist of duties. It describes friendship in its focus on helpful presence. Like God, true human friends faithfully render aid in the hour of need.

- "A friend loves at all times, and a brother is born for adversity" (17:17).
- "A man of many companions may come to ruin, but there is a friend who sticks closer than a brother" (18:24).
- "Do not forsake your friend and the friend of your father, and do not go to your brother's house when disaster strikes you—better a neighbor nearby than a brother far away" (27:10).

Two chief points emerge. First, everyone needs companionship.

Second, the friendship of God manifests helpful presence and self-disclosure. These constitute the core of real friendship. But we must consider the forces that separate men from the friendships they need.

THE PRACTICE OF FRIENDSHIP IN AMERICA TODAY

Unfortunately, our society does not view friendships the way the Bible does. To apply the scriptural principles, we need to understand our culture.

The Ways of Men and the Ways of Women

Unlike most men, women embrace friendship.[8] They are gifted for intimacy (a man might say "wired for bonding"). They seek friendships and work at them. If you doubt this, tour a card shop until you find the section labeled "Friendship." A typical man does not know this section exists because he sends cards only when he must, plucking something from his wife's card drawer if possible. He has never sent a friendship card. Women send cards to each other when there is no birthday, anniversary, birth, or illness to demand it. Friendship cards say, "As I sipped my coffee this morning, I thought of you" or "I am glad you are my friend." (There are no friendship cards for men. No one has ever tried to launch a line of "Buddy Cards." Marketing departments know better.)

Little girls are like their mothers. They hold hands. They talk on the phone about "us." They send notes that say, "You are my very best friend. I love you. Do you love me too?" If little boys sent notes like that, at best their friends would hit them and say, "What's wrong with you? Do you want to wrestle or make a fort or something?"

I do not believe women outdo men in every way. Every good gift can be abused, and women's friendships are no exception. If the male quest for strength degenerates into autonomy and autocracy, the female quest for socialization can lapse into entanglement and codependency. Women can form cliques or become jealous and gossipy. They can become too enmeshed in their friendships. If one becomes miserable, the other *literally* commiserates and becomes miserable

too. Yet, on the whole, women have far more constructive friendships than men, for they care about them more.

Men, by comparison, are careless about friendships, forming
them almost accidentally. When men work or play together, it hardly
matters who their partners are, as long as they are decent fellows
who contribute to the goal. For example, suppose a man (we'll call
him John) goes to a basketball court looking for a pickup game. John
only hopes to get on a decent team, with players who know how to
pass, play team defense, and work together. A few minutes into the
game, John finds that he can already communicate with one teammate (Mike) with a glance, a nod of the head, or single shouted
words such as "Middle!" or "Outlet!" The next week, John is pleased
to be on Mike's team again. The third week, John *hopes* to get on
Mike's team. The fourth week, Mike and John arrange to be on the
same team as sides are chosen. After three months, John and Mike
are talking after the game. After seven months, Mike has to move
away due to a job transfer. The next week John goes to play ball,
without Mike. Then it hits him—"I miss Mike. You know, he was my
friend."[9]

So it goes with men. They work or play with someone for a
while, and one day, months into their relationship, it dawns on them
that they are friends. Sometimes they only recognize a friendship
after it is over. So men fall into friendships almost by accident!

Since men enter into friendships through a shared task, their
relationships are typically *one-dimensional*. At work men talk about
work. In the neighborhood they talk about yards, cars, and barbe-
cues. At church they talk about the faith and perhaps sports or hunt-
ing. At sports events, they talk about the team and the game. Rarely
will men talk about marriage or career in these settings.

I do not disparage one-dimensional relationships. Most of us
know so many people that most relationships *must* be shallow. How
much can we expect from mail carriers, salesmen, and hosts of others with whom we have regular but routine encounters? But something is wrong if a man has nothing but one-dimensional

relationships, if he relates to others strictly according to their functions or roles in his life.

We can explore the problem of shallow relationships by describing four types of friendship between men, comparing them to the
divine standard (that is, the twin traits of *self-disclosure and helpful presence*). Three are flawed. but one shares the marks of God's friendship.

A Typology of Men's Friendships[10]

Good old boys: presence without self-disclosure. Good old boys drink beer
and swap stories at the bar, or in the Christian subculture they meet
at a coffee shop for a few laughs. They often grew up together and
have stuck together through thick and thin. Good old boys are always
there when you need them. They gradually build up a reservoir of stories and inside jokes that get an easy laugh, but they never express
affection or emotion, because "If you have to say it, you don't have
it." To discuss deep feelings is "feminine"—uncomfortable territory.

One-point friends: limited presence, limited disclosure. One-point
friends cooperate to reach a goal in work, sports, or combat. These
men have one thing in common and little more. They work on that
one thing, talk about that one thing, and rarely move beyond it. They
may be very emotional and expressive when they reach their common goals. After winning a big game or sharing a great adventure,
they may think nothing of weeping, hugging, and swearing their
love for one another. But otherwise they literally stay at arm's length.

Leader and follower: one discloses needs, the other gives help. If one man
clearly exceeds the other in a skill or an experience they both treasure,
that man assumes the role of leader. If the men are roughly the same
age, the superior will be "the man" and the inferior his sidekick. If their
ages differ, they may adopt a mentor/disciple pattern. The older man
plays the role of mentor, guide, teacher, sponsor, and role model for the
younger man, who may one day rise to the mentor's level.

Genuine friends: helpful presence and self-disclosure. Genuine friendship may begin as a one-dimensional relationship. But something
happens, and the next dimension opens. Perhaps their wives like

each other. Or they share an aspiration, a vocation, or a struggle. They wonder, *Is there more here than I realized?* Men who care about friendship stay alert for signs of the phase when true friendship can sprout. We can become one-point friends and establish an enriching relationship in a day. But mutual, profound self-disclosure is rarely easy or rapid. It takes time and effort. If one confides while the other shares nothing, the relationship becomes awkward. Self-disclosure entails risk, but the investment is worthwhile.

If you want to pursue a potential friendship, you must make a little time for it. Since time is precious and since men grow together by working side by side, try to take on a project together. Get on the same team. As you help each other, take small steps toward self-disclosure. As friendship begins, you will admire your comrade's strengths. But we seal a new friendship when we see our comrade's flaws and continue to pursue the relationship anyway.

FRIENDSHIPS BETWEEN MEN AND WOMEN

Speaking of the risks of friendship, people often ask whether adult men and women can be friends. Some stress the dangers of temptation and misunderstanding. Yet if we refuse friendships with the opposite sex, we cut off the insights, skills, and excellence of half the human race. Remember, Jesus struck up conversations with women and let them anoint Him, weep over Him, support His ministry, and sit at His feet (Matt. 26:7; Luke 7:37-38; 8:1-3; 10:39; John 4:1ff.). He shattered the standards of His day by treating at least two women, Mary and Martha, as friends.

The rabbis of Jesus' day ordered the separation of the sexes. They thought casual contact between men and women was perilous because they viewed women as empty-headed temptresses whose very presence caused temptation. But Jesus did not blame lust on the mere presence of a woman; lust is an improper response to a woman. Therefore, Jesus spoke to women—even disreputable women. And let no one object, "That was safe for Jesus; He was sinless." Yes, Jesus was (and is) sinless, but He was also a real man, tempted in all things just as we are (Heb. 4:15). Further, He intended His life to be a pattern for ours. He knew that when He decided to associate with women, it signified that male-female friendships are worthwhile, obstacles and temptations notwithstanding.

Friendships between single men and single women run the risk that romantic feelings may stir in one person but not the other. Yet single men and women can carve out safe space for a relationship. The key is open communication and the careful avoidance of mixed messages. For example, if someone *says* they want a strictly "brotherly" friendship, they should *act* like it. Casual friends do not share late candlelight dinners. They do spend time together in groups and public places. A trip to the zoo, with hot dogs and a pretzel for lunch, implies one thing, dinner and a concert another. If romantic feelings rise in only one heart, it will bring pain to the relationship. But if it blooms in both, fine! (There may be wisdom in letting mutual friends help a couple through the awkward time when two people explore the deepening of a relationship.) It is healthy for a romantic relationship to begin as a friendship. The relationship will probably be more realistic, with fewer delusions.

Married men and women can be friends too, within limits. It may start indirectly, through the friendship of the husbands or wives. Eventually the two couples get together and form a foursome. Your friend's wife becomes your friend, and your conversation partner too. When my wife, Debbie, and I have occasionally gone to the house of our friends Steve and Sue, Steve and Debbie, both musicians, sometimes end up by the piano, while Sue and I, both educators, talk about school twenty feet away at the coffee table.

These relationships enrich us at several levels. They provide another perspective on life, another way of seeing things. I also understand my wife better because I have seen her through the eyes of her female friends. Above all, there is the simple pleasure of talking to an interesting person. Of course, it is wise to be cautious, for an element of attraction could enter and cause harm. So a married man should not spend time alone with a married woman (a limit on "presence" in their friendship). They should also avoid intimate topics (modifying self-disclosure) and cultivate a solid friendship between all four parties.[11]

Can a friendship between a man and a woman lead to pain or sin? Yes, but *every* good thing can be abused, whether food, drink, sleep, work, sex, technology, or friendship. The potential for abuse does not rule out the proper use of friendship. We must simply handle it with care.

OBSTACLES TO FRIENDSHIP

Men gain social approval in our culture for being good workers, providers, husbands, and fathers, but not for being good friends. Of course, to be successful at work, a man needs to be *friendly*. Cordial, decent men will form one-dimensional friendships to ensure that phone calls get answered, that vital data and favors flow back and forth at the right time, and so on.

Yet in our culture millions of men are friendly but have no friends. We may have a thousand associates, and fifty of them *could be* friends, but somehow none of them *is* a friend. I call these friendly associations post-it note relationships—joined by a mild adhesive, with a link easily broken. Our society undermines deeper relationships in three ways: 1) misconceptions about masculinity, 2) excessive mobility, and 3) acquisitive culture. Misconceptions about manhood may be the most widespread and destructive.

In chapter 2, we discussed two leading misconceptions—the tough guy and good provider models of masculinity. Because the tough guy endures pain alone and suffers in silence, he projects a self-reliance and self-sufficiency that bars self-disclosure. The good provider's emphasis on earning pushes him to work long hours, leaving no time for relationships. In some cases the good provider's insistence on supplying all his family's needs can have the effect of sequestering women at home, limiting both his wife's relationships and the use of her gifts. More insidious, the good provider model promotes a willingness to go anywhere any time to find a better job. Thus it fosters the dark side of mobility.

Mobility is part of the culture of freedom that Americans treasure, but it destroys friendships by severing the regular contact they need. It ends the joyful retelling of shared triumphs and sorrows—the tales of the big game, the unbearable boss, the impossible task accomplished. Mobility separates friends, and men recover slowly because they hardly try to recover. Mobility encourages rootlessness. As we haul up the anchors of family, history, and tradition, we become vulnerable to the call to reinvent ourselves. Family and friends are thus not there to remind us of the best and worst of who we are.

Mobility is not intrinsically immoral, but wise men know how to resist the careerism and materialism that makes one jump at every offered increase in rank or salary. They buck the egoism that believes the flatteries of strangers who swear, "You are just the man we need." They deflate the naiveté that imagines that the perfect job exists. They also remember how precious friends are, and how rarely friendship survives a passage across the continent unscathed.

Our acquisitive culture also enervates friendship, especially in its links with cars and suburbs. People once found most of their friends in their neighborhood. They bumped into each other at local stores and stopped to chat as they walked tree-lined streets. Now we cruise malls, shuffling past hordes of strangers to fill overstuffed closets. We spend summer evenings holed up in air-conditioned fortresses wired for entertainment. Casual contact with neighbors disappears. The free time we could have is devoured by long commutes and "proper" social activities.

Our acquisitive culture does not just accumulate *things*. We also acquire *experiences* for ourselves and our children. The time we dedicate to the acquisition of experiences can wipe out friendships too. Men can become friends through a youth soccer league, but misguided devotion to children can create false demands for child-development activities. Parents think they must give their children an opportunity to develop every skill and whim. So they spend half their free time running to games or lessons. But children also gain life experience by staying in a room with wise adults and listening a little.

THE PURSUIT OF FRIENDSHIP

We can see why friendship has failed to thrive in Christian communities. Obstacles abound, from careerism to misconceptions about masculinity. Friendship suffers from comparisons to divine love and from the possibility of promoting selfishness. Yet God has ordained it, blessed it, and modeled it as part of a good life. Through friendship we learn to make commitments and stick to them. We learn to listen, to empathize, to expose our dreams and fears to loving scrutiny. Friendship cures the loneliness of the single and the "gender loneliness" of the married. David and Jonathan, Ruth and Naomi show how friends teach each other, how they spur each other on toward good deeds.

Certain spiritual lessons are best taught by friends. Friends warn of hidden weaknesses and encourage hidden strengths. Their confidence impels us to take risks for the kingdom, to uncover buried talents. Friendship provides another source of companionship, taking pressure off marriages. Through their wise counsel and godly example friends help us walk with God. Friendship brings comfort in affliction, partnership in adversity, and joy in companionship. Friends build good lives together. But, men, if you believe all this, you must *pursue* it.

DISCUSSION QUESTIONS

1. How many genuine friendships do you have with men? What do you gain from the friendships you have? What more could you gain?
2. If you don't have good friendships, why not? What can you do to produce deeper friendships?
3. What can you learn from women about friendship? From other men you know?
4. How do you describe your friendship with God? What can you learn from His friendship with His people, as the Bible portrays it?

7

A Man and His Work

Paul Byrd is a devoted Christian who led National League pitchers in hit batsmen in 1999. Byrd is a friend of his former teammate and catcher, Eddie Perez. Perez had already been hit and injured repeatedly in 1999 when Byrd hit him with a pitch in a hot July game. Perez barked at Byrd, but nothing happened until the 185-pound Byrd came to the plate two innings later. As he stepped up, Byrd told Perez he hadn't meant to hit him. Perez, a large man, didn't believe it. He shoved Byrd, then smacked him on the head with his catcher's mitt. Both benches cleared, creating "an angry pig pile" at home plate. Moments later Perez was on top of Byrd, with their faces inches apart at the bottom of the heap. Byrd yelled to Perez, "The Lord Jesus is my Daddy, and He takes care of His children. He knows I wasn't trying to hit you! He's going to take care of me; so you better be careful with me." This startled Perez, whose anger melted away. "Stay with me, Byrdie. I'll help you," he yelled as he threw teammates off Byrd. Byrd stayed in the game and won. Afterward he said, "It's not my intention to hit people, but the Lord blessed me with a short right arm and an 85 mph fastball, and I have to throw inside to win."

This story illustrates key lessons about work. Byrd knows His gifts are from God and that he must use them well. He tried to show integrity in a difficult, public task. He aimed to live by faith at work. He refused to park his faith at the door.

We could learn from Byrd. Some think of work as a purely secular activity, hardly connected to their faith. They know they shouldn't cheat or lie at work. They may share their faith with a friendly seeker; but otherwise, their faith is a private affair. They seldom consider the basic questions about work: How does our faith affect the products we make? The way we market them? Our view of the importance of profits?

The church rarely addresses these questions. Pastors urge us to provide for our families and to keep the Ten Commandments but tell us little more. We are so busy talking about the church and its functions that work is almost forgotten.

We forget that Jesus' first message was, "The kingdom of God is near. Repent and believe the good news" (Mark 1:15), not "Repent, for the church is at hand." Jesus came proclaiming the kingdom, not the church. The church is the vanguard and focal point of the kingdom, but the kingdom is broader than the church. The kingdom of God is the Lord's kingship, His royal reign over all. Because God rules everything, we ought to submit every square inch of life to Him, including our work.

WORK AS DUTY

The Christian man works. Paul said, "If a man will not work, he shall not eat" (2 Thess. 3:10) and "If anyone does not provide for his relatives, and especially for his immediate family, he . . . is worse than an unbeliever" (1 Tim. 5:8). Paul also says *how* to work: "Whatever you do, work at it with all your heart, as working for the Lord, not for men" (Col. 3:23). Earlier Solomon said, "Whatever your hand finds to do, do it with all your might" (Eccl. 9:10).

God also sets a pattern and limit for work: "Six days you shall labor and do all your work, but the seventh day is a Sabbath to the Lord your God. On it you shall not do any work" (Exod. 20:9-10). This law commands both labor and rest. It forbids both ceaseless toil and laziness. The book of Proverbs describes the sluggard: "The sluggard craves and gets nothing, but the desires of the diligent are fully satisfied" (13:4). Proverbs also mocks him: "How long will you lie there, you sluggard? A little sleep, a little slumber, a little folding of the hands to rest—and poverty will come on you like a bandit" (6:9-11).

WORK AS DIVINE ACTIVITY

Because the God of the Bible works, work is divine activity. He plans, creates, and fashions reality. He places birds and colors in the sky above and animals, plants, and minerals on the earth below. He called worlds into life, then formed and arranged them to declare His glory (Ps. 8:3; 19:1). When He finished, He rested, establishing the cycle of work and rest. He still tends and oversees His creation (Ps. 104:10-22). In Scripture, God compares Himself to a gardener, a potter, a shepherd, a farmer, a builder, a garment-maker, a tentmaker, and a king.

Jesus also works, with delight, saying, "My food is to do the will of him who sent me and to finish his work" (John 4:34). He works as long as there is light; His work had an urgency to it (John 9:4). The Father delighted in the work of creation and judged it "very good." The Son also took satisfaction in His task—redemption. When He completed it, he declared, "It is finished" (John 19:30).

So work is a God-like activity. Godly men share the Lord's positive attitude toward labor. We are glad to do His work, accepting His commission to govern creation for Him. We are the king's vice-regents, the president's vice presidents.

At its best, the boundary between work and play fades as pleasure in our work reflects God's pleasure in us. Vigorous work and vigorous play both demand singular concentration. When we do the right thing the right way at the right time, it nourishes us. When we finish what God designed us to do, it does not drain us but strengthens us. When we concentrate on God-given tasks, using God-given abilities, we are close to Him. We bless ourselves and mankind. The hours fly by. Work becomes collaboration with God. Nehemiah described this beautifully when he told how the Israelites rebuilt the wall around Jerusalem. First he says, the wall went up because "the people worked with all their heart" (Neh. 4:6). Later he says the wall went up because the "work was done with the help of God" (Neh. 6:16). This sense of participation lets us pray to God, "Establish the work of our hands" (Ps. 90:17). "Unless the LORD builds the house, its builders labor in vain" (Ps. 127:1).

WORK AS CURSED ACTIVITY

But work is not always so noble. It brings frustration and drudgery. We sometimes doubt the Bible's lofty ideals regarding work. Look at the bored faces of janitors, cashiers, and assembly line workers. Many of the most repetitive tasks have been taken over by machines, but laborers still have to tend them. One worker put it this way:

> Put it on, take it off. Put it on, take it off. In between I don't even try to think. If I were to put you in front of a dock and pulled up a skid in front of you with fifty hundred pound sacks of potatoes and there are fifty more skids just like it, and this is what you're gonna do all day, what would you think about, potatoes? . . . A mule, an old mule, that's the way I feel.[1]

Tedious as that sounds, that cannot compare to the lot of laborers in undeveloped nations. In India I saw a group of workers move the dirt for a four-story building by digging with hand shovels, loading the dirt into straw baskets, hoisting them onto their heads, walking a quarter of a mile to a landfill, dumping them, and walking back. Of course, they could not afford earthmoving equipment, but why no wheelbarrows, I inquired. If they purchased *good* ones, my host replied, they would be stolen immediately, and poor ones are worthless. Besides, efficiency is not the Indian way, he continued. There is not enough work for everyone. It is better if everyone has a job, however menial.

In the beginning it was not so. God mandated work before the Fall, before Adam and Eve rebelled. But when sin entered the world, work became toil—sweat of the brow and the frustration of thorns and thistles. Now sin pervades our work. Cars built on Monday mornings may suffer from hangovers. Projects completed Friday afternoon suffer from hastiness. Sin means many people cut corners as they produce goods and deceive potential customers. It means large companies seek to destroy small ones, perhaps *because* they have better products. The combination of ignorance and malice brings many sorrows.

Most of us have experienced the curses of work. My summer jobs in my school years motivated me to seek a professional—that is, dirt-free—career. I dug potatoes by hand under a blazing summer sun. I washed dishes in such heat and filth that I dreamed of being promoted to busboy. I painted houses, unloaded trucks, put on roofs, tended machines, and knocked holes in walls to earn a dollar. The details may be different, but we all know work can be hot, dangerous, backbreaking, demeaning, and, worst of all, boring. But white-collar life brings little relief. The form of the frustration changes, but not the reality.

The Fall taints work at home too. Developers scrape off topsoil and sell or discard it, and so we have to grow everything in pots. If we do have good soil, bugs and rodents eat our gardens. Sometimes most of our work strives to reverse effects of the Fall.

Fallenness is more than things going wrong. It includes confusion about the right goals for our work. We misjudge our gifts and calling. We become obsessed about finding the right job, about using our gifts, about avoiding predictable frustrations. Yet we invest our energies foolishly. I know a Christian lawyer who became a successful action novelist after years of fruitless late-night writing. His first project, still unpublished, was a novel about World War II fighter pilots. When that novel was rejected by every possible publisher, he began working on a sequel! One might ask why a man would write a sequel to a novel no one would ever read. Yet it took this brilliant man six months to ask himself that question and to start a different book, which has sold very well.

Even when we do succeed, sin leads us to misconstrue our success. We become proud of ourselves, envious of our rivals, and greedy for our gain. Solomon said:

He who loves money will not be satisfied with money; nor he who loves wealth, with gain: this also is vanity. When goods increase, they increase who eat them; and what gain has their owner but to see them with his eyes? Sweet is the sleep of a laborer, whether he eats little or much; but the surfeit of the rich will not let him sleep.

—ECCL. 5:10-12, *REVISED STANDARD VERSION*

PAST THOUGHT ABOUT WORK

A first step in offering our work to God is to think about it correctly, rather than letting the latest management theory or decree from the boss toss us around. Given that the nobility and futility of life so clash in our work, we sorely need pastoral guidance. Sadly, the history of thought about work offers inconsistent help.

Our answers to the fundamental questions about life, about God, and about work are bound together. We ask: Who am I? Why am I here? What is wrong with this world, and how can it be fixed? What are my duties? What is the meaning of human history? Is there a God? If so, what is His nature? Our view of God shapes our opinion of work, and our view of work affects our idea of God. Those who despise work are apt to imagine that God does too. But if the living God works and designed mankind to work, then we should esteem it. God is pro-work; but to grasp the biblical view of work, we must first see why many despise it.

THE GREEK VIEW OF WORK[2]

To the Greeks and certain Romans, "work was a curse and nothing else," an unmitigated evil to be avoided at all costs. Most Greeks believed that work at crafts, trades, or farming lacked nobility. It robbed men of time for friendship and citizenship. According to Hesiod, work originated with Eris, the goddess of strife, and labor came from Pandora's box as a punishment from Zeus. Cicero deemed work unworthy and sordid. The Greeks viewed work as a burden fit for brutes and slaves. Like beasts, laborers enter the world, reproduce, toil, and die, leaving no mark of their presence. The Greeks valued the contemplative life and freedom from bodily necessity. Most placed little value on physical life. But because we have bodies, we must feed them, clothe them, and care for them until they expire. Our bodies enforce an endless cycle of labor. Therefore, the fortunate have slaves to care for them, and their toil gives freedom to nobler men.

The Greek gods both reflect and foster the Greek antipathy toward work. The gods of mythology were idlers, not workers, taken up with their pleasures and occasional forays into the affairs of mankind. Aristotle's god was the unmoved mover, thought thinking thought. So the Greeks despised work.

MEDIEVAL VIEW OF WORK[3]

Ancient and medieval theologians gave scant respect to work. Most of them were preachers or monks whose goal of life was the contemplation of God. Because the active life hinders contemplation, spiritual men left the world and lived in monasteries, focusing on God in prayer and meditation. The monks worked to keep their bodies alive, to prevent idleness, and to discipline themselves. The spiritual value of work was that its pain and humiliation crushes pride and promotes penance. They also thought works of charity toward the poor were virtuous. Such sacrifices please God, they said, give them merit, and help them obtain salvation.

Medieval Christians believed work was an *instrumental* good. It fed the body, humbled the soul, and pleased God. But for them, work had no *intrinsic* value, no direct ability to edify. This disrespect for work had two sources. They accepted much of the Greeks' disregard for bodily life, and they had confused ideas about salvation. They believed God is gracious, but they also thought they had to complete His grace by adding *their* works of charity and devotion.

It is easy for us to criticize these ideas, but we have our own ways of separating faith from our work. Many of us hardly think about the connection between our work and our faith. Christians resolve to tell the truth, keep promises, and avoid work on Sundays. But their faith hardly touches their business decisions about the products they make or the way they sell them. Thousands of Christians produce, market, and sell tobacco, alcohol, lottery tickets, even pornography without asking themselves if that is a proper way to earn their bread and use their gifts.

Too many of us think we practice our faith when we *go* to church on Sunday but forget that we *are* the church every day. We are God's representatives, the vanguard of His kingdom. We must be faithful citizens of that kingdom in our work. If you do not know how to incarnate your faith on the job, at least pray and seek like-minded believers so you can spur one another on.

RENAISSANCE AND REFORMATION VIEWS OF WORK

Renaissance Christians had a clearer view of God, and a better view of work followed. They called God a cosmic craftsman, not a passive, distant mind. He displayed His wisdom and power by creating the universe. Renaissance thinkers called God the "Divine Artificer," the "Supreme Maker," the "Mightiest Architect." As a result, they honored craftsmanship, industry, profit, and labor, not just contemplation. Giordano Bruno thought work was good because it made men develop their creative capacities, which would eventually lead them to exercise control over the earth and fulfill the mandate God gave Adam at creation. The Renaissance denied that work is bestial, for animals work without thought or variation, according to rigid patterns of instinctive behavior. But men use imagination. They plan and execute. They innovate, fabricate, and amend the material of nature. Thus our work is beast-like in some ways, but God-like in others.[4]

The Reformation took the affirmation of work one step further. Martin Luther declared that the farmer shoveling manure and the maid milking the cow please God as much as the minister preaching or praying, if they serve faithfully. God ordains the varied vocations or "stations" of life that men and women occupy. In them we become the agents of God's loving, providential care.[5] Through men's hands, as they work, God answers the prayers of His children. We pray for our daily bread at night, and bakers rise in the morning to bake it. We pray for safety in travel, and mechanics fix cars and planes. When we faithfully discharge our vocations, the naked are clothed, the hungry fed, the sick healed, and the ignorant educated. Work pleases God and strengthens us, but we do not work to earn God's favor or to humble our soul by it. Rather, by our work we love our neighbors as ourselves.

Calvin and the Puritans agreed that men please God when busy in honest secular callings. Indeed, every task, however sordid, is precious in God's sight if it is our calling.[6] Some lines of work are not honest, of course. Christians should not become mercenaries or gamblers or accept any other calling that requires sin. Yet Calvin believed we honor God when we design, manufacture, distribute, and sell. Calvin believed God is active and effective, not just a god dwelling in solitary self-sufficiency.[7] Therefore, he said, we honor Him by our activity at work, by *making* things.

Calvin was himself an entrepreneur. He took an active role in Geneva's government. He offered tax and property benefits to lure cloth manufacturers to the city to alleviate the employment problems of the Protestant refugees who streamed into the city from France.[8]

The ideas of Calvin and Luther remain central to a Christian concept of work. Both men refused to split life into sacred and secular activities. Both stressed our ability to honor God in daily tasks. Satan deceives men, Calvin said, into thinking God does not pay attention to little things, to our labor and housework. Routine work is proper in this life. We serve God even in routine activities. By working, we provide for our families but also bless mankind.

There were differences between Calvin and other Reformers. Luther and most Puritans believed social structures were nearly immutable. They urged men to serve in the place or class given by social custom. But Calvin added that society as a whole can be reformed. We should attempt to reform social structures to promote justice, for *society* is fallen, and not only individuals.

Bad social structures make it harder to live righteously. However tender a slaveholder might be, the *system* of lifelong slavery gives owners an unwarranted level of control. Similarly, caste systems organize prejudice and domination. In America today, extreme inequality between school districts makes it hard for poor parents to educate their children properly. Some experts believe current systems of transportation favor the affluent suburbs at the expense of inner cities and rural areas.

The Reformers made two crucial claims. First, no workplace is utterly secular. However degraded a place may be, God claims it. Second, He reforms us through our work. These principles enable us to live like His children in the workplace and to exercise His reign there.

THE GRANDEUR AND THE MISERY OF WORK

Because God works and intended mankind to work, even before sin entered creation, we should have a guarded optimism toward work. Jesus worked with His hands, with building materials. By working with His hands, He dignified all manual labor. (Dare I say he was a construction worker?)[9] The Gospels confirm Genesis: God created all humans in His image, so that men from every station in life are honorable. God treasures the working poor, the dishwashers and housecleaners who perform the humblest tasks. God knows no caste system. He chose lowly shepherds as the first witnesses of the Incarnation. Jesus' friends included fishermen and tax collectors. All honest work possesses value in God's sight.

Greek theories of work are quite different. They think manual labor and poverty shameful. They deny that any God created mankind in His image. They deny that everyone possesses dignity. Of course, the Greeks were not entirely wrong. Labor can humble and afflict us. The misery of work explains why certain men start dreaming of retirement in their forties. We need a critical realism. Sometimes our duty to provide for our families pushes us into difficult positions.

- To provide for his family, an aspiring songwriter may become a sound technician. A struggling professional athlete may go into coaching.
- We may find ourselves in a dishonored occupation. Every year pollsters list the most and least respected occupations. Medical professionals and teachers always lead the list of heroes, and lawyers, insurance agents, telemarketers, and used car dealers head the list of villains. But Christians need to stay in dishonored (but not sinful) occupations too, to bring God's truth to bear on them. Surely society needs more honest lawyers, insurance agents, and used car dealers!
- We get drafted into positions we would never choose, but the Lord uses us there. Because God gave him the power to interpret dreams, Joseph became Pharaoh's second-in-command and saved many lives.

Beyond all this, our economic systems also seem to foster certain problems. Slave economies debased both slaves and masters. Communism fostered indigence. Patronage systems instill corruption. The free enterprise system can reduce workers to a kind of commodity as they sell their time and skill to the highest bidder. Loyalty between employers and employees erodes.

But there is good news too. The Bible is not exactly pro-business, but it does promote a robust attitude toward work. God filled the world with resources and charged mankind to nurture and develop them. Because God works and plans, we can plan too. Further, the variety of human gifts teaches us to live in a society of mutual dependence, bound by mutual needs and services. Each man assists his neighbors according to his God-given talents.

Some important work garners no wages—for example, volunteer work and housework. Because work is more than a livelihood, many continue to work even after they retire. Work gives us meaning and direction, identity and purpose. Through work, we gain the satisfaction of contributing to something larger than ourselves. The joy of producing and achieving explains why some retired men work as hard as ever at investing or restoring old cars.

Admittedly, many work because they conform to roles society imposes on them. Society rewards workers and punishes slackers. But we do more than gain wealth and social status through our labor. Work is tainted by the curse and the irritation of working with other sinners. But it still has intrinsic value because God works and summons us to be His fellow-workers. Still, to gain the most from work, we must discover our gifts and calling.

Work in a Blessed Calling

Colorado has a camp called Horn Creek. Perhaps its greatest attraction is Horn Peak, rising to 13,500 feet, 5,000 feet above the main lodge and eight miles distant. One summer a small group climbed it, and somehow I became a lead guide as we made an ascent that is more arduous than dangerous. Unfortunately, "leading" meant keeping up with four athletic teenagers, including my daughter Abigail. We made it to the summit despite howling winds that buffeted us and threatened to toss us off the final ridge, far above the tree line. When we reached the top, I was tired, and not just because I had hiked an 11,00-foot peak the day before. During our descent, a rock gave way under my daughter. She sprained an ankle, and we had to carry her the last three miles to camp. Three men helped, but a father's sweat is less odious than a stranger's, so I did the lion's share of the work. At 120 pounds, she is big enough that I wanted to start a chorus—"She ain't heavy, she's my daughter." It was hot, exhausting work, but, honestly, I did not have a more satisfying afternoon all summer because I love hiking and I love my child. Work is not burdensome when you do what you love for those you love.

But how do we find the right work? How do we discover the divine design, our place in God's plan? How do we distinguish God's voice from our desires, whether for prestige, possessions, or perks? The historic Christian answer begins by distinguishing two kinds of calling: our universal calling and our particular calling.

Our universal calling is God's summons to everyone to believe in Him, to repent of sin, to know, trust, and follow Him (Rom. 8:28-30; 1 Cor. 1:9; Gal. 1:6, 15). Our universal calling includes the privilege of reflecting God's character in all things. Paul says God calls us to conformity to the Son (Rom. 8:28-30), calls us to peace (1 Cor. 7:15), calls us to freedom (Gal. 5:13), and calls us to be holy (Rom. 1:7).

But God also prepares us for a *particular* calling. It begins with genetic gifts and predispositions given before birth. It continues with His providential care as He shapes us through our parents, teachers, friends, and employers. God leads us to our occupations, even to individual jobs. The Bible describes this as a calling too. Paul said he was called to be an apostle. God called Jeremiah, Isaiah, and Ezekiel to be prophets. By listing apostles and prophets first, I do not imply God only calls men into what some call "full-time Christian service." Not at all. We can even serve God when called as slaves (1 Cor. 7:21-22).

Dedicated Christians who labor in business or the trades need to digest this. Many of them suffer a vague sense of guilt. They think their work stands one notch below pastors or missionaries who "serve the Lord every day." Every year a few such men come to seminary because they love God and want to serve Him. Their church has not sent them, and they are not equipped for ministry, but they come, thinking that everyone who truly loves God must serve Him in "full-time ministry." In fact, the noblest thing we can do is to serve the Lord faithfully in the place to which God assigns us. A so-called "secular" calling can be full-time service too.

Most of us exalt some occupations over others. Christians typically honor pastors. Secular people may honor political service. A couple of years ago, the tax return of a wealthy politician disclosed that he had donated only $600 to charity in an entire year. When asked why he was so miserly, he replied, "I have given my life to public service." I wonder, does he think bakers, truckers, farmers, garbage collectors, and secretaries do *not* serve the public? We may not extol political service, but many Christians share the belief in higher and lower callings.

But before God, all honest callings are noble. Cashiers, execu-

tives, and pastors are alike before God. Of course, Christians must
not choose illegal or immoral work. But we can serve God in any
legitimate vocation. Indeed, the highest position anyone can hold is
the one to which God has gifted and summoned him.

I could not have written this book if I did not believe that. For
several years I served Covenant Seminary in three roles at once—as
professor of New Testament, vice president for academics, and dean
of faculty. But I resigned the vice presidency, though it had the highest prestige, pay, and rank, to serve where my greater gifts lay—in
teaching and writing. Just as important, God prepared my successor
to be a better administrator than I am.

This does not mean we can pursue whatever we choose. First,
too many people want to be professional athletes, musicians, and
artists. No matter how strong our desire may be, we are not called to
an occupation if no one ever offers us a job in that field. Second, God
may summon us to difficult tasks that deprive us of the peaceful pursuit of our preferred activities. Third, a man must pursue a career that
lets him provide for his family. A friend once stood at a crossroads
between two careers—concert pianist and investment banker. He is
a gifted musician, but he chose investment banking because the
prospect of providing for his family through music was so uncertain.
Investment banking is his *vocation* while music is his *avocation*.

FINDING GOD'S CALLING

How do we find our vocation? How do we know when it is time to
take a new position, whether to provide for our family or to meet
important needs? The Bible does not directly address these questions
because in biblical times people did not have the options we enjoy
today. Most people were farmers or herders, and most pursued their
parents' vocations. Still, we can list a few principles.

First, consider what people actually invite you to do. Of course,
not every invitation stems from perceptive judgments of our skills.
But wise men and women often see our gifts better than we do. They
ask us to do what they see us doing skillfully. Second, our calling is

usually also something we desire. So ask yourself: What do you love to do? When do you feel pleasure in your work? When do you feel *alive*? What work would you do for free if wealthy? When do hours of work seem like minutes? Of course, every job has its burdens, but we tolerate them if we spend most of our time using our chief gifts. Third, where do you bring the greatest help, the greatest blessing, to others? If all three principles converge, your calling is probably there.

- An internal aspiration, with the necessary preparation.
- An external verification: Employers or customers will pay you a living wage for your services.
- An external result: The fruit or success that satisfies workers, employer, and customers.

On the other hand, we are tense and frustrated when our work runs against our grain. We feel miserable when no one wants the services we want to offer. We wonder, *Am I blind or are they?* The unemployed struggle, in part, because they wonder why no one wants what they offer.

Centuries ago sages counseled fathers to take children who sought a calling on tours to visit men working in various trades—to the sea for sailing, to the garrison for soldiering, to the church for ministry. As they walked through markets, farms, and shops, parents watched for sparks of interest. The child picked something and tested the work. The work also tested the child. Thus good parents detected and promoted the inclinations of their children. Today friends can do something similar for each other.

CONCLUSION

Work is complicated. Its riddles seem all the more intense because work is so essential to our lives. It is both exalted divine activity and repetitive human duty. The frustrations of work make our fallenness so clear. Yet our glory emerges in our achievements at work. If men can think more clearly about their work, perhaps they can find their callings and enjoy God's blessings there.

DISCUSSION QUESTIONS

1. Is your view of work more like that of the Greeks, the medieval theologians, or the Reformation? What are some consequences of failing to view work from the proper perspective?
2. Do you ever have the experience of gaining strength from your work? How often does your work make you feel alive?
3. Do you agree that no job is entirely secular? How does that conviction affect your work? Do you work for God's honor and kingdom while you labor?
4. Do you have a lingering suspicion that "full-time Christian service" is slightly superior to all other callings? How would you answer your own doubts about the value of "secular" callings?
5. Do you believe your current job is God's calling to you? What do people ask you to do? What do you love to do? Where do you bear fruit?

8

A Man as Leader

Martin Luther once said, "Young fellows are tempted by girls, men who are thirty years old are tempted by gold, when they are forty years old they are tempted by honor and glory."[1] Luther understood that for many men, leadership is a temptation before it is a calling. Many of us associate leadership with higher pay, more respect, and a nicer office at work. Even in the church, we link leadership with honor rather than character. Once, at a conference in a small town, I asked my host, obviously a respected leader, what made people respect a man in his town. He replied, "A man knows he's got it made when he has a good truck, a cabin on the river and the office of elder in the church. . . . Of course, if he can kill a deer with a bow at fifty paces, that helps too." Valued skills, possessions, and positions are the currency that buy us social respect. But Luther knew, as we do, that Jesus defines leadership differently:

> *"You know that the rulers of the Gentiles lord it over them, and their high officials exercise authority over them. Not so with you. Instead, whoever wants to become great among you must be your servant, and whoever wants to be first must be your slave—just as the Son of Man did not come to be served, but to serve, and to give his life as a ransom for many."*
>
> —Matt. 20:25-28

Even in the business world, leadership ought to be—perhaps it must be—hard work and service first, long before it ever leads to glory. Before he reached national fame, Sam Walton used to dress in blue jeans and a flannel shirt, drive up to his Wal-Mart stores in a pick-up truck, and buy light bulbs, shampoo, and toothpaste, just to make sure his customers were served properly. Of course, to discover the true level of service in his stores, he had to go unrecognized. Walton understood that to lead, you have to serve, and to serve you have to forego glory sometimes.

Beside its interest in servant leadership, the Bible stresses character-based leadership. The key text for that is 1 Timothy 3, Paul's description of a church elder. Of course, leadership in business and society is much broader than authority in the church. Nonetheless, Paul's principles apply to every kind of leadership.

The Character of a Christian Leader

If anyone sets his heart on being an overseer, he desires a noble task. Now the overseer must be above reproach, the husband of but one wife, temperate, self-controlled, respectable, hospitable, able to teach, not given to drunkenness, not violent but gentle, not quarrelsome, not a lover of money. He must manage his own family well and see that his children obey him with proper respect. (If anyone does not know how to manage his own family, how can he take care of God's church?) He must not be a recent convert, or he may become conceited and fall under the same judgment as the devil. He must also have a good reputation with outsiders, so that he will not fall into disgrace and into the devil's trap.

—1 Tim. 3:1-7

Notice that Paul's list first describes the *character* of an elder, not his work. Paul begins, "The overseer [an elder] must *be*," not "An elder must *do* . . ." Of course, all leaders must have skills and personal strengths. Fittingly, Paul mentions the ability to teach and manage. But all other elements of Paul's list refer to personal qualities, not tasks. Thus Paul calls oversight "a noble *task*," but he emphasizes the leader's character more than his skills. This is especially striking since Paul calls the church leader an "overseer" here. *Overseer* is interchangeable with *elder* (cf. Titus 1:5, 7), but it usually refers to a leader's *functions*, whereas *elder* refers to his maturity. Paul seems to be saying, "Your first 'function' is to be mature." For a Christian, it is not enough to do the work—we must also be a God-made man. Paul explains three aspects of a leader's character in Timothy: his virtues, his family, and his reputation.

THE PUBLIC VIRTUES OF A LEADER

At first glance, Paul's list of virtues has little in common with other New Testament virtue lists. He does not mention Christian virtues such as love, faith, righteousness, or endurance. Of the fruit of the Spirit listed in Galatians 5:22-23, only one of them, self-control, also appears in 1 Timothy 3. But if we look more closely, we see that while the words differ, almost every *concept* from the list of the fruit of the Spirit appears somewhere in the traits of a leader here. Specifically, the list in 1 Timothy 3 describes the fruit of the Spirit as it expresses itself in public. The *public* behavior of a leader in family, church, and society proves that God is working in him privately, internally. The chart below compares the ninefold fruit of the Spirit (Gal. 5:22-23) to the traits of an elder (1 Tim. 3:1-7; Titus 1:5-9).

The Fruit of the Spirit	Traits of an Elder
Love	Elders take care of family and church, an expression of love (1 Tim. 3:4-5).
Joy	Joyful people are contented, and hence free from greed for money (3:3).
Peace	Elders are not violent or quarrelsome (3:3).
Patience	Elders are not quick-tempered (Titus 1:7). Patience aids teaching (1 Tim. 3:2; cf. 2 Tim. 2:24-25).
Kindness	Hospitality (1 Tim. 3:2) publicly expresses kindness.
Goodness	Every term in the list is a form of goodness. Titus 1:8 says elders "love what is good."

Faithfulness	Elders are faithful to wives and children and to the faith (1 Tim. 3:2; Titus 1:9; cf. 1 Tim. 3:9).
Gentleness	Elders are temperate and gentle,[2] not violent or quick-tempered. Gentleness is also part of the aptitude for teaching mentioned in 2 Timothy 2:24-25.
Self-control	This is the one word or phrase that appears in both passages.

The results are clear. Paul expects leaders to experience the fruit of the Spirit and to express that fruit publicly. But a leader must show his character in the world, not just in the church. Paul shows that he knows this by placing several key *pagan* virtues in his list.

THE PAGAN VIRTUES OF A LEADER

My phrase *pagan virtues* may sound like an oxymoron, and indeed the Greco-Romans, for example, often lived by standards we find appalling. For entertainment, they watched gladiators fight, even to the death. In some temples, "worshipers" copulated with "sacred" prostitutes. In Ephesus, a brothel stood directly across the street from one of the ancient world's largest libraries. But not everyone was amoral. Many pagans prized the cardinal virtues of courage, justice, wisdom, and temperance. Both ordinary citizens and moral leaders admired generosity, insight, and self-control.

Paul's description of a leader in 1 Timothy 3 shows that he treasured some of the same virtues that pagans valued. He mentions *temperance* and *self-control* (discussed above) in 1 Timothy 3:2. He forbids elders to love money and enjoins hospitality (3:2-3), showing his approval of *generosity* and the popular view that wealth is to be shared, not hoarded. We conclude, therefore, that *elders must meet the valid pagan standards of the day*. That is, the public conduct of Christian leaders must be acceptable to pagans who, by God's grace, make some accurate moral judgments.

We must handle this principle carefully. First, I do not imply that noble pagans lived up to their high moral ideals. Second, we do not follow pagan standards; we follow biblical standards, giving thanks that some pagans accept them to some extent too. Nonetheless, in every generation some secular people admire many of the same moral qualities that we admire. Today morally sensitive pagans have a high regard for honesty, financial integrity, marital fidelity, generosity, and hard work. Consider how much Christian leaders such as Billy Graham have enhanced their ministries by shining in these areas. And consider how much the cause of Christ has suffered when fallen ministers exposed themselves to society's proper disdain for fraud, deception, hypocrisy, and infidelity. For the sake of its credibility, church leaders should meet the valid pagan standards of the day.

CHARACTER TESTED

Good leaders are strongest in times of severe testing. They are ready to fight where the battle rages. They engage the issues of the hour. When crises arise, they lead the way when others get lost. Thus Paul required leaders to be strong precisely where the false teachers who troubled the church were weak:

- The false teachers were violent and quarrelsome (1 Tim. 6:3-5; cf. 2 Tim. 2:23). But an elder teaches all gently and kindly and avoids quarrels (1 Tim. 3:3; cf. 2 Tim. 2:24-26).
- False teachers love money (1 Tim. 6:5, 10). But leaders are generous and hospitable. They neither love money nor dishonest gain (1 Tim. 3:3; Titus 1:7; cf. Acts 20:33).
- False teachers love speculation, breed controversy, and "do not know what they are talking about" (1 Tim. 1:6-7). But leaders know what they believe and can teach it (1 Tim. 3:2, 9).

Leaders also persevere. Observe that the list in Titus describing those who *will be* elders and the list in Timothy describing those who *are* elders are virtually the same. This means that becoming a leader is not like cramming for an exam. True professionals, whether in medicine, law, finance, or technology, know they must keep improving their skills; they cannot study and forget. Likewise, leaders cannot cram for character, then forget it. If anyone thinks that way, Paul's letter thwarts them. He gives the leader's character requirements. By announcing the list publicly, Paul lets the whole church, even the whole world, call leaders to account.

So leaders prove themselves *publicly* by their exemplary character. They also prove themselves *privately*, in their families. Jesus said that if someone is faithful over small things, He will entrust them with larger things (Matt. 25:21-23). If a man cannot love and care for his own family—a few people, whom he knows best—how can he manage a larger family, the church? Leaders prove they can lead in a large arena by leading well in a smaller, easier arena, the family. Paul mentions both marriage and parenthood in his teaching about leaders in 1 Timothy 3. Both comments are short but rich.

THE MARRIAGE OF AN ELDER: LOVING A WIFE AND LOVING WOMEN

Paul's first remark, that an overseer must be "the husband of but one wife" (v. 2), seems clear, but there has been considerable debate about Paul's precise message. Literally, the Greek (*mias gunaikos andra*) says an overseer must be "a one woman man." This short remark can mean one of four things:

Option 1: Paul believed overseers had to be married men. Of course, most Christian leaders are married, but why would Paul make this an absolute requirement? After all, he was single himself, and he was an overseer of the church. Further, Jesus, the supreme leader of the church, was unmarried. Furthermore, Paul commended celibacy for those with such a gift because it increases freedom for service (1 Cor. 7).[3] So Paul must have meant something else.

Option 2: Paul believed overseers may marry only once in a lifetime. That is, any man who has divorced and remarried cannot be a Christian leader. Certainly divorce is a great evil, and the leadership potential of an adult Christian is gravely damaged by it. But the problem with the once-in-a-lifetime view is that it also forbids widowers from marrying, and that seems like a gratuitous legalism. The Bible elsewhere grants widows and victims of infidelity the right to remarry (Rom. 7:2-3; 1 Cor. 7:8-9, 15, 39; Matt. 19:8-9), and Paul would not contradict that.

Option 3: Paul believed overseers must be monogamous. This is certainly true. But polygamy was already illegal in the Roman Empire, and almost no one practiced it. Why would Paul bother to forbid a sin no one committed? Again, he must have had more in mind.

Option 4: Paul believed overseers must be faithful husbands. Leaders must be monogamous, but more, they should be exemplary husbands. This makes sense in both Paul's day and our own. A similar passage in 1 Timothy 5:9 supports this view. There Paul says a widow who receives financial aid from the church should have been "the wife of one husband" (RSV).[4] In context, this clearly means she was a *faithful* wife. Here, at last, a familiarity with country music promotes Christian thinking. Paul is describing what country music would call "a one man woman," as in the song "I was a one man woman, but he was a two timin' man." When Paul requires a leader to be "the husband of but one wife," he means he should be a "one woman man," that is, a faithful man.

From time to time a man sidles up to me and complains, "I just don't understand women," as if his ignorance of the female species accounts for his marital woes. But this is a mistake. Husbands, Paul does not ask you to understand women as if they were a field of academic study. You must know and love and serve *one woman*, your wife, working to understand her and to use your knowledge in order to love her in every way. After that, perhaps you can try to understand, love, and serve the other women God places in your life.

THE CHILDREN OF AN ELDER: LEADING CHILDREN AND LEADING THE WORLD

Paul also expects leaders to prove themselves with their children, as they manage and take care of them (1 Tim. 3:4-5). To "manage" (v. 4) is to oversee, direct, and plan the things that involve or affect his family. To "take care" (v. 5) is to lead by serving everyone, by nurturing the weak and forgotten ones, by going last.

Notice that Paul does not simply require leaders to have obedient children. The children should obey *"with proper respect,"* with dignity. That is, parents ought to *obtain* obedience without shouts or threats or violence, and children ought to *render* obedience respectfully, without slouching, grumbling, or rolling their eyes.

Parents of teens may think this is like asking for a snowball fight in the Sahara Desert. But we can gain obedience with respect if we have a proper relationship with our children. Infants and little children submit to their parents out of necessity. They are utterly dependent on their parents, who are so big and strong that the youngsters often have no choice but to obey. If we tell a twenty-month-old, "Time for bed" and he yells, "No bed, no bed!" all we have to do is pick the boy up, put him in the crib, pull up the side, turn out the light, and shut the door. But the older children get, the more independent they become.

Older children might still submit to unloving parents because they know they need them and because they fear punishment. If parents show that love motivates the laws and chores of the household, older children might obey. But they might not obey with a submissive, respectful spirit, especially as they become teenagers.

Mao Tse-tung was right when he said, *"Power* proceeds from the barrel of a gun" (emphasis mine). That is, people will obey when someone points a gun at them. But what happens when the gun—the threat of punishment—is removed? People obey when compelled, but then they rebel as soon as they can. On the other hand, if leaders exercise what I call *"intimate* authority," people follow willingly. That is, teenagers (and adults) give obedience with respect when they recognize both the *position* of the leader and the leader's *right* to it. We have the right to govern when we are duly appointed, by God or man, to a position and when we use our position for the good of others.

Children of all ages are much more likely to submit willingly if they know their parents lead with love, with justice, and with their good in mind. Herb Kelleher, the founder and CEO of the immensely successful Southwest Airlines, won legendary loyalty from his employees by slinging luggage alongside his ground crews and serving drinks with his flight crews. In contemporary companies, workers love it when the CEO's office and furnishings are only slightly nicer than theirs. They love it when everyone contributes, everyone has a voice, and everyone gets a vote, even if somehow the boss always has the decisive vote.[5]

Likewise, the effectiveness of church leaders depends more on the care they give than on the power they wield. Church and family are so similar that if you cannot lead the latter, you cannot lead the former. Both require direction from the top down and service with a humble attitude, even from leaders. Good leaders neither shirk leadership, nor use it for selfish advantage.

Some husbands and fathers suffocate their wives and children through ungodly domination. Others abdicate their leadership role. Domination may be the greater error, but abdication is the more common error. Too many men are too lazy, too exhausted, and too distracted to lead. Everything I just said about husbands also applies to leaders.

Children respond to parental authority when parents lead by example, when they give reasons for what they say, when they appeal to the imagination, not just rules. Then they obey with respect. Adults are the same, only more so. We respond when we see a servant at the helm, not just a boss. Of course, the boss can dress down, play volleyball, and make hospital visits to create a veneer of egalitarian concern. But many of them mean it, and their leadership makes an impact. Christians take their cue from Jesus, who didn't just dress down for company picnics. He dressed down to wash His disciples' feet, even though He saw no immediate rise in their productivity. He suffered Himself to be dressed down further still by the Romans at His crucifixion, though He gained no personal benefit from it. By His sacrifice He redefined leadership and inspired new levels of loyalty and obedience.

A few years ago my family witnessed a remarkable example of Christlike, redefined leadership. My daughter Abby joined her high school's cross-country team the fall of her freshman year. The team was strong, and she expected nothing more than an opportunity to meet people and get in shape. But as the season progressed, she surprised everyone by coming in toward the top of freshman races, then junior varsity races. In the last regular-season race her time bested a couple of experienced varsity runners. With district and state championships coming up, the varsity runners asked the coaches for a team meeting and asked Abby to join it. One of the seniors told the coach, "We have all seen that Abby has been running really well lately, and we think she deserves to run on the varsity for districts." She paused and looked at Abby, then at the coach, caught her breath, and concluded, "And she can have my place."

For the sake of the team, that runner gave up her last two varsity races. Coaches love to talk about senior leadership, about players stepping up to take the lead. But in this case stepping down was leadership. I wonder where we would be if Christian leaders were so secure in God's love, so sure of their identity in Christ, that they too could give up their place and put others first. When people know their leaders are willing to put them first in this way, it becomes so much easier to follow. Spiritual authority depends more on care given than on power wielded.

Like John the Baptist, true leaders know when to say, "He must increase, but I must decrease" (John 3:30, RSV). As the hymn says:

> I would not have the restless will, that hurries to and fro
> Seeking for some great thing to do, or secret thing to know. . . .
> I ask thee for the daily strength, to none that ask denied . . .
> Content to fill a little space, if thou be glorified.

ANNA WARING,
"FATHER, I KNOW THAT ALL MY LIFE"

REPUTATION

Finally, Paul considers the public standing of a leader. First, Paul forbids that an elder be a recent convert (3:6; literally, "a newly planted person"). Paul does not specify how long someone must be a

Christian before becoming a leader, but the metaphor of a growing plant suggests that maturation is a process that cannot be rushed. It is not the style of Paul or of the Bible overall to specify a timetable for leadership. Still, we can say it *ordinarily* takes at least a few years for someone to gain sufficient maturity to lead. Christians certainly find reasons to rush new converts into leadership: We don't have enough leaders; our current leaders are weary; new Christians have enthusiasm; we want them to grow through service. But Paul says a hasty rise to prominence tempts us to give in to pride and conceit. This leads to "the condemnation of the devil" and "the snare of the devil" (vv. 6-7). This can mean one of two things. Either pride will trap immature, conceited leaders so that they share the condemnation the devil must endure. Or the devil will use the immature leaders' pride to trap and condemn them. Whichever Paul means, we should want no part of it.

It is better if people slide into leadership gradually. If someone has ability and humility, he will seek to *assist* first. If, as Jesus said, he proves faithful in small tasks, then he can take charge of more (Matt. 25:20-23). To put it differently, the best way to find new leaders is to locate people who are already leading quietly but effectively in little noticed corners. There are exceptions, but if God has called and gifted someone to lead in an area, He has probably placed a desire for that work in their hearts. Therefore they will find a way to become active in that area, even if no one recruits or rewards them. On the other hand, once someone becomes known, it is worthwhile to observe what others ask them to do. Communities are usually very good at reading the skills of their members. If someone is being asked to organize events over and over, they are probably good at organizing. Conversely, we can discover the sphere where we may best lead by asking, "What do people most regularly invite or recruit me to do?"

Paul also requires leaders to have a good testimony or reputation with outsiders (3:7). This is fitting, since he already insisted that elders meet the valid pagan standards of the day. But why does Paul again emphasize this matter of reputation? Above all, we must recognize that nothing undermines the church's witness faster than the loss of ethical rectitude. Secular people already have a certain antagonism toward the church for claiming high standards, for a perceived "holier than thou" attitude. We probably all know a Christian businessman—perhaps you are one of them—who cannot fit in with "the boys" when a work team travels out of town. The guys are out gambling or womanizing or drinking at a strip club while he stays in his room, reading and watching TV. His wordless testimony may make them hostile or derisive or uncomfortable or all three. Is he "holier than thou"? In a way, we cannot avoid that accusation. We *do* lay claim to a high standard. We *do* aspire to holiness, and if someone else cares nothing for holiness, then we *do* try to be "holier" than others. Of course, once we make the claim, the world will do us the honor of holding us to it.

Bill Clinton inadvertently illustrated this point at the beginning of his presidency. When he ran for president in 1992, he promised loudly and often to restore the highest standards of ethical rectitude in his administration. After the election, Clinton nominated Zoe Baird, a lawyer, to be attorney general, the nation's highest law enforcement officer. Married to a constitutional lawyer at Yale, Baird's family enjoyed an income of $600,000 annually. Soon, however, she disclosed that she had hired illegal aliens to watch her child—a special embarrassment because the attorney general oversees immigration. Further, despite her income, she had also dodged Social Security contributions for them for two years. Finally, she had the gall to blame her errors on bad legal advice. The public exploded, and with calls flooding into senators' offices to oppose her nomination, she withdrew.

So Clinton proved that those who *claim* a higher standard will be held to it. Because Christians claim a higher standard, our leaders must have a good reputation. To be sure, reputations are not always accurate. Yet, in the long run we usually get a reputation that is close to what we deserve. The inner man shows himself often enough that our reputation at least roughly matches our character.

Conclusion

In review, Paul's description of a Christian leader looks daunting. First, a godly leader should experience the fruit of the Spirit and, second, demonstrate that fruit publicly. Third, he should meet the valid pagan standards of the day. Fourth, he is strong wherever spiritual battles rage. Fifth, he is a dedicated husband. Sixth, his children render respectful obedience. Seventh, he has a good reputation in his community.

We are all so flawed that we wonder, *If this is the standard, who deserves to lead?* But Paul does not mean to disqualify leaders. Rather, he describes who *is* qualified, whose life and aspirations make them leaders. In some ways the Bible is simply describing a Christian man with normal maturity. It just seems demanding because most of us fall so far short of God's patterns.

So then, what does God require of the man who wants to be a fruitful servant and an effective leader in His kingdom? One must be a Christian, must know his sin, must know Jesus is his only hope, now and forever. All leaders have certain gifts that they are willing to hone and use, especially when it is difficult to do so. Public leaders need gifts of mind and tongue and social relations. One must have a call and the spirit to follow it. But I believe the Bible says here that what an elder needs most is the desire to serve, not a thirst for honor. Gifts are important, but for the Christian leader there is no substitute for godliness and a willingness to work where the work needs to be done.

Discussion Questions

1. Have you thought of leadership as something we do more than who we are? Why is Christian leadership more a matter of character than deeds?
2. Are you a godly leader in the home? A one-woman man? Do you lead and care for your children?
3. Explain the difference between authority and power in the task of leadership.

4. Are you mature enough to lead? Is your reputation good enough? Why does that matter? Is your walk of faith deep and long enough? Do you aspire to godly leadership? For the right reasons?

5. Do you lead in the social or public spheres? Do you serve in difficult places? If not, what prevents you from expressing your faith in public arenas?

9

A MAN AND HIS WEALTH

The value of the dollar slowly spirals downward, but North Americans never seem to tire of the question, "What would you do for a million dollars?" My favorite is an old poll in *USA Today*. Forty-two percent of the respondents said they would do at least one of the following: spend two years in jail, permanently move to a foreign country, never see their best friend again, throw their pet off a cliff (we had a parakeet at the time!). What would *you* do for a million dollars? Perhaps you think the question is beneath your dignity. Perhaps you think you are too contented, too principled, to succumb to such crass temptations. But Jesus thought otherwise.

A QUESTION OF MONEY

One day Jesus was teaching a crowd about the cost of discipleship. Men can kill our bodies for following Him, He said, but we should fear God, who can cast body and soul into Hell. Yet if we remember and confess Him, He will confess us on the last day (Luke 12:1-12).

One can hardly imagine a weightier discussion, but a man in the crowd interrupted as soon as Jesus paused. "Teacher," he blurted out, half pleading, half demanding, "tell my brother to divide the inheritance with me" (v. 13). We do not know if this man had actually suffered an injustice, but he believed his brother had taken too much.[1]

Jesus replied brusquely, "Man, who appointed me a judge or an arbiter between you?" (v. 14). In fact, the man did have reason to call on Jesus. He correctly viewed Jesus as a teacher, and Israelites turned to teachers, not lawyers, to resolve their disputes. But Jesus declined to play the judge. It was not His mission to settle family disputes; indeed, sometimes He causes them (vv. 51-53). Jesus refused to give the man what he *asked*, but he offered what he *needed*—namely, a better understanding of possessions.

THE DANGER OF GREED

Jesus began with a double warning: "Watch out! Be on guard against all kinds of greed; a man's life does not consist in the abundance of his possessions" (v. 15). Twice the Lord tells the man to beware ("Watch out! Be on guard"), for greed is a subtle enemy. Whether we have much or little, even if we have shunned the paths that lead to a large income, greed can infiltrate our souls. We can become greedy if our neighbors have more than we do or if we meet an old friend who has done a bit too well. We all have days when possessions seem very important—too important.

Imagine the life of Leonard, a college freshman whose year has come and nearly gone without a single solo encounter with a young lady. Pondering his plight, he decides the problem is transportation. *If only I had a car*, he thinks, *I would have a social life.* Since Leonard is a Christian, he prays for a car, and God answers—with an old Volkswagen. But it is neither fashionable nor reliable. What girl wants to go on a date knowing there is a 15 percent chance of walking back? Frustrated, Leonard prays again. "Lord, thanks for the car, but I need something more dependable." Again God provides—a fifteen-year-old economy car. It runs, but the previous owners' children were known to dump milk in the air vents. Mix this with the aroma of partially burned oil circulating through the rust holes in the back, and Leonard still has no social life. He prays again. "Lord, thank You for providing, but I know I could find the girl of my dreams if I had something a little more sporty." This time he finds a ten-year-old sports car. It *is* sharp, but it gets only seven miles per gallon, and the insurance costs $4,700 per year. So he cannot afford to drive it. Resolute, Leonard prays again. "Lord, now I realize that I need a newer, more economical car." You get the point. Leonard has slipped into believing that the right possessions *do* grant the good life.

Adult men rarely fix on one thing they must have. Instead they focus on the income stream that provides every need and an array of desires—finer clothes, finer foods, and exotic vacations. "If only my boss paid me what I'm worth, if my business were more profitable, if the stock market were more stable, then I could afford a bigger house, a real vacation, a nicer neighborhood. Then we would be content." Indeed, financial security makes us feel peaceful, and the increase of possessions brings a temporary lift.

Yet as income increases, so does outgo. Whatever we have, we always crave more. Ecclesiastes says, "Whoever loves money never has money enough; whoever loves wealth is never satisfied with his income" (5:10). Gathering possessions to find contentment is like drinking water to satisfy hunger; it stops the aching for a while, but it cannot solve the root problem. Still hungry, we crave more; since we choose the wrong remedy, our appetite remains. "The eye never has enough of seeing, nor the ear its fill of hearing" (Eccl. 1:8). Wealth cannot satisfy our deepest longings. As Solomon says, "I denied myself nothing my eyes desired; I refused my heart no pleasure. . . . Yet when I surveyed all that my hands had done . . . everything was meaningless" (Eccl. 2:10-11).

Once after I gave a talk on money, a middle-aged man approached me, smiling sadly. "I am making twice as much money as I ever dreamed possible, but I find that it still isn't enough," he confessed. Jesus understands that. He knows the subtle threat of greed, and He told a parable to show that life does not consist in the abundance of possessions:

> *"The ground of a certain rich man produced a good crop. He thought to himself, 'What shall I do? I have no place to store my crops.' Then he said, 'This is what I'll do. I will tear down my barns and build bigger ones, and there I will store all my grain and my*

goods. And I'll say to myself, "You have plenty of good things laid up for many years. Take life easy; eat, drink and be merry."' But God said to him, 'You fool! This very night your life will be demanded from you. Then who will get what you have prepared for yourself?' This is how it will be with anyone who stores up things for himself but is not rich toward God."

—LUKE 12:16-21

A FOOL AND HIS MONEY

At first glance this parable seems poorly matched to the concerns of the man who was worried about his inheritance. Outwardly the man in the crowd and the man in the parable are opposites. One does not have enough possessions; the other has too many. But inwardly they share a hidden commonality, a solidarity discovered by listening carefully to the farmer.

At first Jesus' farmer looks like an honest man. Since God gives fruitfulness to the earth, the man's wealth seems to be a token of God's blessing. His ground produced a crop so bountiful that he had a storage problem. Surveying his crop, he proposed a solution: "I will build bigger barns." He will make an investment to protect his assets; that looks like good stewardship.

But after he makes his plans, he dreams his dreams, and we see another side, a side that is not so innocent. Once those new barns are complete, he will "take life easy; eat, drink and be merry." Alert readers notice that he exemplifies the hedonist credo, "Eat, drink and be merry, for tomorrow we die." The farmer's hedonism is rather obvious, but he has a second problem that emerges if we paraphrase his speech a bit, emphasizing the pronouns:

He thought to himself, "What shall I do? I have no place to store my crops. Then he said, "This is what I will do. I will tear down my barns and I will build bigger ones and there I will store all my grain and my goods. And I will say to myself, "Self, you have plenty of good things laid up for many years. You take life easy. You eat, you drink, you be merry."

This strange-looking paraphrase follows the original, where eighteen of the farmer's fifty-four words are to or about himself.[2] Notice, too, that the bulk of the parable is a monologue. This also seems innocent, until we notice whom he does *not* consult. The farmer does not pray about his wealth; he neither thanks God nor seeks His direction. He does not confer with friends or family about his possessions. He has no thought of sharing with the poor. He talks *to* himself and *about* himself, which is suspect in itself.[3]

The farmer thought he had a storage problem. He proposed an architectural solution—bigger barns. He hoped that would guarantee that he would enjoy his possessions for many years. Indeed, the farmer believed life *does* consist in abundant possessions. In his soliloquy, he planned to keep his wealth for himself. He thought he was alone in his room, but to his surprise, someone else was there—God—and He interrupted the farmer's plans.

God called the farmer "You fool" not because the farmer was stupid, but because he said in his heart, "There is no God" (Ps. 14:1; 53:1). The fool need not be a philosophical atheist who believes he can disprove the existence of God. As long as he is a practical atheist, a fool may vacillate on the existence of God. Practical atheists do not care if God exists or not because they think that even if God does exist, He sees, knows, and does nothing.

The fool in Jesus' story anticipated many years of ease, but he forgot God and forgot the coming day of reckoning. He trusted a dead god—money—and that resulted in his death. The living God told him, "This very night your life will be demanded from you. Then who will get what you have prepared for yourself?" (v. 20). The farmer wanted to guarantee his possessions for himself, but he forgot that "Naked a man comes from his mother's womb, and as he comes, so he departs. He takes nothing that he can carry in his hand" (Eccl. 5:15; cf. Job 1:21). One day God will demand an accounting. We will have to account for the use of our material wealth as well as the gifts of mind, energy, or artistry God has given us.

The word translated "demanded" deserves our attention too. It means to "recall" or "ask back" something that was stolen or loaned out. That is, God will "recall" our lives as a lender recalls a loan. Our life and possessions are not truly ours; we have them on loan.

On Loan from God

We typically view both our wealth and our abilities as *our* possessions. We think of *my* organizational skills or people skills, *my* intellect, artistry, or athleticism. When I exercise those abilities well, I earn *my* money. In a way, our abilities do belong to us. But surely we know that most of them were bestowed at birth. Yes, we hone skills and practice them, but who implanted a desire to hone them? Who sent a coach or teacher to direct our development? Deep within, we know all our abilities are gifts and loans from the Lord, given for His pleasure, not just our own.

I am writing this page during a busy week. Saturday I presented a seven-hour seminar. Sunday I preached and taught Sunday school in a large church. Monday I lectured for four hours in regular classes at Covenant Seminary and led a devotional for a student group. Tuesday I led a Bible study for 120 men and lectured two hours for a colleague who had an appendectomy. Wednesday, after a regular class, I preached in chapel at 10, led a discussion on mentoring at noon, and lectured on parenting at 7, covering for my pastor. By Friday the total will be twenty-six talks.

This passage keeps my attitude right. I could pity myself: "Why did people get sick and go away in such a busy week?" I could berate myself: "Why did I accept all these requests? Why did I arrange my schedule so poorly?" I could boast: "See how everyone turns to me in time of need?" Instead, I need humble gratitude. Of the week's talks, seven were fill-ins, five on short notice. My friends called me because they know I can craft cogent talks in a hurry. So I plunder an old lecture, adding one section, deleting another, sketching introductions and illustrations as a useful (not to say great) talk rapidly emerges. This odd little skill of sketching talks rapidly has always been there. I never sought or honed it; I take no pride in it. But perhaps God takes pleasure in watching me print pages of notes, snatch them off the printer, dash out the door, climb in the car, and try to jot organizing remarks at red lights. When I speak, my introduction flops, but I gather momentum as I career through my notes. It isn't artistry, but it's edifying. God must smile in pleasure at this odd use of His gift.

I wish every man could perform an inventory and see his abilities as *God's* gifts and loans. Each of us has abilities that are simply there. They earn us praise and money, but they are God's more than ours. Since our gifts are His loans, we should "be rich toward God" (v. 21) with all we receive for exercising them. Jesus tells us how to do that. "Give to the poor" and put your "treasure in heaven," He declares (vv. 33-34). Being rich toward God might mean:

• Supporting an inner-city church plant, so it can afford the staff it needs—a pastor, musicians, youth workers, literacy workers, job trainers.

• Giving Bibles and basic reference works to students bright enough to enter a premiere Asian Bible college but poor enough to be unable to afford one book.

• Buying a motorbike for an African pastor exhausted from walking ten to fifteen miles daily between the seven churches he serves as preacher, teacher, and counselor.

• Putting off the renovation of your basement so you can pay for room, board, and tuition for the child of a church planter who serves a village in India too small to support a school of its own.

Being rich toward God means gently leading your wife and children to see that an old car can be viewed as an embarrassment or as a gift to the kingdom. If you have $40,000, which is the nobler use—to purchase one "cool" vehicle or to provide a *century* of food, clothing, and Christian education for impoverished children overseas (ten children for ten years each at $400 per year)? Being rich toward God means deferring or eliminating some expenses so you can tithe, and more than tithe. It means celebrating when you reach 15 percent. It means fixing our eyes on the things that matter to God, even if they have no publicity office.

The farmer understood none of this. Because he saw only *his* possessions, it seemed logical to spend them on self-indulgence. This is precisely how most people—even Christians—think. "My skills and my hard work earned me *my* money." But God says the skills and the funds are both His, loaned to us for a season.

This is not an attack on the rich, for Jesus targeted wealthy and poor alike. The man in the crowd and the rich farmer were *financial opposites but spiritual twins*. One had too little, and one had too much, but both believed life *does* consist in abundant possessions. Both were fools. Both needed to be rich toward God. Yet neither could do so, for they loved money rather than God. Only a God-made man can use money God's way. For all others, wealth is a rival deity. As Jesus said:

> *"Do not store up for yourselves treasures on earth, where moth and rust destroy, and where thieves break in and steal. But store up for yourselves treasures in heaven, where moth and rust do not destroy, and where thieves do not break in and steal. For where your treasure is, there your heart will be also. The eye is the lamp of the body. If your eyes are good, your whole body will be full of light. But if your eyes are bad, your whole body will be full of darkness. If then the light within you is darkness, how great is that darkness! No one can serve two masters. Either he will hate the one and love the other, or he will be devoted to the one and despise the other. You cannot serve both God and Money."*
>
> —MATT. 6:19-24

WHOM DO YOU LOVE?

This teaching stands near the climax of the Sermon on the Mount. There Jesus described the life of discipleship and warned about idols such as reputation and money as they try to displace the Lord. The statement, "Do not store up for yourselves treasures on earth . . . But store up for yourselves treasures in heaven" is both command and battle cry. The command is, "Don't store treasure on earth because here it rots and in Heaven it is worthless." The battle cry is, "Depose the blasphemous deities!"

Indeed, everything decays under the assault of moths, rust, water damage, and inflation. Therefore we should store treasures in Heaven, where they are safe, guarded by the God who also guards us. Placing treasure in Heaven means investing in God's causes and God's people. Do that, and your heart will follow, so that both heart and treasure are safe with God.

Pagans cannot grasp the lesson of Matthew 6. Atheists cannot store treasure in Heaven. If there is no God and no Heaven, it is nonsense to think about storing anything there. Secular people *inevitably* store their treasures on earth. How could it be otherwise? They cannot trust God to reward them when they deny His existence. Unbelief destroys the capacity to obey.[4]

In the verses 22-23 Jesus drops talk of treasure and Heaven and speaks of eyes and light. The theme seems new, but actually it is a new perspective on the same issue. In the Bible, the "eye" and the "heart" can both refer to that inner core of a person that sets his life's direction.[5] When Jesus says "the eye is the lamp" (v. 22), He means we find our way through life by the direction it gives, whether good or ill.

Jesus' diagnosis of us is: "If you cannot take your eye off your wealth, if you live for it, it is because your eye—your heart—is corrupt!" If our eyes are dark, there is no hope, unless God grants renewal. No one can *do* what is right unless he can *see* what is right. The unbeliever inevitably hoards treasure on earth because he neither sees nor knows the Father in Heaven. Therefore, Jesus does not tell the unbeliever, "Try harder to store treasure in Heaven." He says, "Examine your heart, your eyes."

Jesus focuses on unbelievers, but He warns disciples about greed too. We see this in the specific Greek words used for the good and bad eye. Literally, "If your eyes are bad" (v. 23) reads, "If your eye is *evil*." And literally, "If your eyes are good" (v. 22) reads, "If your eye is 'simple.'"[6] In biblical times, "evil eye" signified a jealous eye, a coveting eye. Thus, while Jesus tells unbelievers to examine their eyes, He warns disciples against jealous eyes. Instead of jealous eyes, we should have simple eyes. A simple eye is clear; it does not see and covet—it simply sees. A simple eye is generous because it is not always seeing an angle. When it gives, it just gives. It does not give *and* ask what is gained by the gift, what favor may be returned. It has no ulterior motives.

We must be careful where we set our eyes. When visiting a prosperous friend, watch your eye as you scan his beautiful possessions. At home, beware of mail-order catalogs with their exquisitely textured but too expensive fashions. When car advertisements find you, *don't* picture yourself behind the wheel. Beware of gracious living magazines; they may provoke jealous schemes to get everything in them. The graphic display of the body to promote sensual lust is called pornography. I believe we also need a word for graphic displays of wealth designed to promote materialistic lusts. *Plutos* means wealth in Greek; so perhaps we should call it plutography.

To unbelievers, Jesus asks in essence, "If you cannot control your eyes, what is the reason for your inability? Go to the root of the matter—your allegiance to other gods." To believers, He warns, "Be careful, little eyes, what you see." He concludes:

> *"No one can serve two masters. Either he will hate the one and love the other, or he will be devoted to the one and despise the other. You cannot serve both God and Money [Mammon]."*

"Money" is capitalized because Jesus labels it a god. Some translations render this "Mammon," which means "that in which one trusts."[7] Indeed, we are prone to trust money. Remember the prayer, "Give me neither poverty nor riches. . . . Otherwise I may have too much and disown you and say, 'Who is the LORD?'" (Prov. 30:8-9; cf. Hos. 13:6). Jeremiah commands, "Let not . . . the rich man boast of his riches" (9:23). And Ezekiel accuses, "Because of your wealth your heart has grown proud" (28:5). Job knew that a man can speak to gold and say, "You are my security" (31:24). David sang, "Though your riches increase, do not set your heart on them" (Ps. 62:10).

Yet we do trust in riches. Our words prove it. America's national retirement plan is called "Social *Security*." We call our investments "securities" and "trusts," as if we can trust them for a secure future. We also make money a god in additional ways. We give it the title of deity: "the Almighty Dollar." We make money a judge. When someone asks, "What is he worth?" he or she means, "How much money, how many assets, does he have?" We speak as if a man's financial assets determine his worth.[8]

Of course, money is not the kind of god that explicitly demands exclusive worship. No one needs to get on his knees, for money is a *polytheistic* deity. It merely wants a shrine somewhere in the pantheon, one with room for other demigods, such as status, power, and pleasure. It even lets its worshipers be Christians too.

These ideas baffle some people. They cannot see why they must choose between God and Money. They think it quite feasible to serve two masters. They honor God for part of Sunday, serve Mammon Monday to Friday, and reserve Saturday for themselves. They may even think that God and prosperity go hand in hand. But they are thinking of faith as a hobby, like gardening. Or they regard God as an employer, not a master. Surely a man can *work* for two employers, schedule permitting. But no one can *belong* to two masters. No slave can be the property of two owners, "for single ownership and full-time service are of the essence of slavery."[9] We can serve either God or Mammon but not both.

THE RICH EXTERMINATOR

Few people openly live for money, but I did encounter one while in seminary. Hoping to find a summer job to cover the next year's tuition, I searched for seasonal work that was unpalatable enough to pay well and chose pest exterminating. After calling several businesses, I got an interview with a young and energetic owner. He shook my hand, sat me down, then asked, "What is your purpose in life?" Momentarily stunned, I soon seized this surprising chance to share my faith and launched an explanation of a Christian's life purpose. Sixty seconds later the exterminator interrupted me. "Listen, my purpose in life is to make money, and I want to know if you want to make money." At one level, I understood him. After all, does anyone start a pest control business in Philadelphia out of a generalized love for humanity?

The exterminator had exceptional clarity, but not exceptional convictions. Candid and self-aware, he announced, "I live for Mammon." Many people do, but they prefer to mask it. They like shades of gray, not black and white. The gray palette lets them say, "I look at my house, my car, and my furnishings as investments" and "I simply want to provide the best things for my children."

Jesus presents a stark choice between two ways of life. Will we store treasure on earth or in Heaven? Will our eyes be light or dark? Will we serve God or Mammon? He addresses both rich and poor, for both want "just a little more." Both seek security in material wealth. Rich or poor, Christian or pagan, all are susceptible to greed.

Sadly, most Christians live roughly like their peers, even if those peers are pagans. If the careers and income are the same, the lifestyle is probably the same too—the same hours of work, the same use of money, the same overstuffed schedules. Our vision of the good life owes more to society than to Scripture.

We can always explain our behavior away: "We work hard and only want our due." "Others have much more." "God wants to give gifts to His children." "We will be good stewards of our possessions." And so on.

The poor strive to get what they can. The rich spend or hoard to guarantee their future security. North Americans are nearly the richest people on earth, but studies show that American Christians give about 3 percent of their income to charity, including the church, mission work, and all the rest. Sadly, as they grow richer, people usually donate *lower* percentages of their wealth. Somehow we convince ourselves that we are deprived whenever we cannot get what we want. We compare ourselves to someone who has more. We run after possessions like the pagans, but nothing satisfies for long.

RICH TOWARD GOD

The cure for the malady of materialism is generosity toward God, starting with the heart, then moving to actions. Generosity of heart starts with trusting God rather than worrying about food or clothes. Jesus supplies four reasons not to worry (Luke 12:23-29). First, God feeds birds, and we are more valuable than they (v. 24). Second, worrying is futile. Worrying cannot add one hour to our life (vv. 25-26). Third, God clothes wild flowers and grasses with beauty, though they last but a day, and we are more valuable than they (vv. 27-28). Fourth, God knows our needs and will supply them if we seek His kingdom first (vv. 29-31). Knowing this, disciples can sell their possessions and give to the poor (vv. 32-33). As one scholar said, "Serious application of this principle to contemporary churches would require such radical transformation of most Christian fellowships that few seem willing even to begin." But great journeys start with a single step. Some fear schemes to redistribute wealth, but we could travel far down that road "before anyone suspected us of extreme obedience."[10]

FOUR WAYS TO BE RICH TOWARD GOD

Use money as God directs. Paul lists three proper uses of money in 1 Timothy. First, to meet basic needs for food, clothing, and shelter. "If we have food and covering, we will be content with that" (6:8). Second, to enjoy God's good creation. "God . . . richly provides us with everything for our enjoyment" (6:17). Third, to give generously. "Those who are rich in this present world [should] be generous and willing to share" (6:17-18).

Develop a godly career. A few biblical laws govern our careers. First, we must work to supply our needs (2 Thess. 3:6-10). Second, our work should be constructive and lawful. No Christian should work as a thief, gambler, or pornographer. Third, we should do good to all, offering them something of value.

More than laws, we need godly goals for our careers. We should offer our work to God, governing our corner of creation for Him, using the gifts He bestows. One day we will stand before the Lord and render an account. Who wants to say, "Lord, I used my business skills to market fake fireplaces." Instead, let us strive to use the highest gifts God grants us. At the same time, we must guard against overwork and organize our careers to retain time for family, friends, church, and godly pleasures. We must refuse to work seventy hours per week just to support expensive tastes.

See wealth as God does. "Everything God created is good" and to be "received with thanksgiving" (1 Tim. 4:4-5). Yet Christians should never be engrossed with money (1 Cor. 7:31-35). The Bible never condemns those who *are* rich. Abraham, Joseph, David, Solomon, Jehoshaphat, Josiah, Job, and Joseph of Arimathea were all rich and blessed by God. But Scripture often warns us against making it our life goal to get rich. "The love of money is a root of all kinds of evil" (1 Tim. 6:10). People who live to get rich love this world, not God. They fall into temptations, traps, and snares. If our gifts and efforts lead to riches more or less by accident, praise God. But we should not choose a career just to get rich (Jas. 4:1-4; 1 Tim. 6:6-10). Riches are a good servant but a bad master. There is more profit in contentment whether we have much or a little.

Pray for a generous heart. My wife and I learned in seminary that one need not be rich financially to be rich toward God. We arrived in January with no job. After paying tuition and rent, our wallets were as barren as the winter landscape outside. Our meager savings dwindled for five weeks as neither of us found work. It could have been frightening, but God sent us a seminary couple with generous hearts. We knew them from college, and when we arrived, they invited us to dinner. When they learned that we had no income, they invited us to dinner again days later. Every few days they invited us again. When we asked them to a meal, they laughed. "Not now; invite us over when Debbie gets her job." Objectively, they didn't give us much. Seven meals in five weeks cannot stave off bankruptcy. But when we lay in bed at night, wondering about our future, our friends' generosity looked like manna, like God's sign from Heaven. One of us would ask, "Will we go hungry?" The other would reply,

"No. God will take care of us. He already sent us Mark and Adele." Small gifts, given with liberality, accomplish great things.

Large gifts are strategic too. Generosity is a spiritual gift (Rom. 12:8). Generous people understand that quotas, like tithing, can impede true generosity. If people tithe to keep a legal formula, they may think, "I gave my due; now I'm done." But Jesus is the model for giving, and He gave all, not just 10 percent. Generous people *love* to give. They taste the splendor of Christ's kingdom, its world-changing power. They see Jesus binding Satan. They delight to support His work in areas where money can make a difference.

CONCLUSION

This age keeps its eye on money, but the man after God's heart keeps his eye on God and His kingdom. He knows he cannot serve both God and Mammon. He realizes that all he has is a loan. Beyond the tithe, he sets the generosity of Jesus as his model. Because his heart is right, God's man is free to be generous. Generosity is a spiritual gift, and because we love God, we can shake off greed and possessiveness and act generously. If first we are rich toward God with heart and mind, generosity with our wealth follows.

DISCUSSION QUESTIONS

1. Why are we prone to think that life does consist in having the right possessions?
2. What was the rich farmer's basic problem? How does that problem manifest itself today? What forms do "bigger barns" take today? How might we hoard money for our selfish indulgence? Where might the "Eat, drink and be merry" credo show itself?
3. Why do so many people think they *can* serve both God and Mammon? What would you say to someone who seemed to be trying to serve both masters?
4. How can you show, by concrete action, that you see your money and gifts as a loan from God?

PART 4

THE MAN OF GOD AND HIS PERSONAL LIFE

10

A Man and His Play

The award-winning movie *Chariots of Fire* tells the story of two runners in the 1924 Olympics. Harold Abrahams is a serious runner. Long before it became standard, Abrahams and his coach analyzed, dissected, and reconstructed his running style to achieve a tiny advantage that would lead to victory in the 100-meter dash. In the film when his girlfriend, who senses his joylessness in the sport, asks why he runs, he replies, "I'm more an addict. It's a compulsion really, a weapon." An English Jew, he ran for Britain, not from love of running, but to prove his worth and to overcome anti-Semitism. The Olympics are not fun; they are agony. In the film, hours before the Olympic finals, he tells his coach and confidant, "I have ten lonely seconds to justify my existence." In real life, he said that just before the race he felt "like a condemned man feels just before going to see the scaffold." Setting a world record, Abrahams won his race and gained the social acceptance he sought. A little while later he sustained an injury and quit running. It had achieved its purpose.

The second runner, Eric Liddell, smiled and laughed as he ran, drinking in its pleasure even in fierce competition. Liddell and his sister Jenny were Scottish Christians dedicated to mission work. In the movie Jenny fears that Eric's love of running will lure him from that commitment. One blustery day they go for a walk, and Eric pledges that he *will* go to China for missions. Yet, to her dismay, he declares that he has a lot of running to do first. He explains, "Jenny,

you've got to understand. I believe that God made me for a purpose—for China. But He also made me fast. And when I run, I feel
His pleasure. To win is to honor Him." Liddell wins too, the 400-
meter dash, then returns to China as he said he would. But once
there, he continued to run, for pleasure.

The story of Abrahams and Liddell illustrates both the joys and
the riddles of sports, exercise, competition, and play. Games are supposed to bring joy and "recreation" (re-creation) to its participants.
At best, we engage in play for the pure pleasure of it. Then God
delights in our delights; our "lawful pleasures" are his.[1] Yet, for too
many of us, sports and games have become a mirthless exercise.
Competition brings out both the best and the worst in us. As we
strive to prove and improve ourselves, we subject ourselves to pressures that are too much like work.[2]

Play is more than sports and competition. It can begin with one
squirt of a water pistol and end with water hoses blasting everyone
in sight. It includes a child playing house and a family playing keep-
away with a ball in a pool. It includes the silly games fathers make
up, games like Tickle Button, Gatekeeper, Crab Arm, and Monkey
Baby.

For some decades now, western societies have had the wealth to
liberate leisure activity as never before. But we find that having fun
can be complicated. We feel that we ought to have more leisure, but
we seem to have less. When we do have free time, we cannot decide
what to do with it. There are two models. In the Greek ideal, leisure
time is dedicated to self-improvement—ennobling music, literature,
exercise, and contemplation. In the Roman model people passively
watch "attractions." If we are Roman, the critics are right when they
say that mass entertainment serves to anesthetize us to the pain and
emptiness of daily life.

The Greek view can lead to leisure that feels a lot like work. But
the Roman view can lead to leisure that looks a lot like waste. And
just as the Romans perverted their leisure with gladiatorial games
and other debasing entertainments, we degrade ourselves with
depraved television shows and movies, not to mention pornography.

The Colosseum's masses cheered injuries in battles, but we injure ourselves with "recreational" use of alcohol, drugs, and sex.

People think about sports, competition, rest, leisure, games, and exercise more than ever these days, but I want to focus on play. Play is part of sports, competition, and the rest, but it is narrower and purer.

THE DEFINITION OF PLAY

"Play is a *voluntary* and *absorbing* activity engaged in for the enjoyment it gives" without regard for the results.[3] "Voluntary" means we cannot *force* someone to play. The statement "I don't want to play" has a certain finality.

"Enjoyment" means play is an attitude. Two children can rake the same leaves, but if one frowns and rakes to finish his chores, he works. If the other smiles and heaps up foliage so he can dive into it momentarily, he plays. When we play, it's safe to make mistakes. After all, it's only a game. Play absorbs us, not because something depends on it, but because it is delightful.

"Absorbing" means the whole person—body, mind, and emotions—participates in play. Play offers wholeness for adults who perform mindless physical work or disembodied mental work all day. By engaging both mind and body, play refreshes and enlarges the spirit.

"Without regard" means that while play produces clear benefits, we don't play for the sake of the benefits. When we play bucking bronco at home or volleyball on the beach, we do not calculate whether the expenditure of time and effort matches the benefits. Play stands outside the normal world of clocks and calculations. Time seems suspended when we play. Sometimes we lose track of it; sometimes it seems to stand still. It sometimes makes sense to hurry at work, but not at play. Hurrying would ruin everything. Play is meaningful in itself. It justifies and rewards itself. Play does have benefits. It pushes us to explore the world and to form bonds with new people. Play offers a respite from the tyranny of work and routine. Peak performances even give us a glimpse of perfection, of eternity, and pitiful performances make us yearn for perfection in a very different way. But that is not why we play.

THE PURITY OF PLAY

There is nothing quite like play. Play shares features with sports, competition, and exercise. It overlaps with rest and leisure, but there is nothing exactly like play.

Play is often athletic, but not all athletics is play, and not all play is athletic. Sport is not always playful. Sometimes the exertion (think of marathons) and the business end (think of salary negotiations) of sport suffocate the enjoyment. When we play, we are supposed to smile and laugh, but during competitive sports we keep our game face on.

We usually exercise when we play, but we can play without exercising and exercise without playing. We play board games and play make believe, but neither one is exercise. On the other hand, exercise includes running, weight lifting, aerobics, martial arts, and calisthenics. Like play, they are voluntary, but we call them "working out," not "playing out." We rarely joke around as we're lifting weights (unless we pervert them—for example, by lifting light weights and pretending they are heavy). We rarely exercise for its own sake; we do it for an end, to stay fit or recover from an injury.

Play is relaxing, but not all relaxation is play. To sit by a stream or go for a walk is relaxing, but not play. Play is participatory. You ordinarily need a partner to play (at least a computer program).

Play is fun, but not all fun is play. Entertaining movies, stirring athletic contests, rides at an amusement park, and witty television programs are all fun, but spectators are not players. Play is active and participatory.

Work has playful moments, but work is not play. Work can have some of the traits of play. We can have fun, get exercise, and become utterly absorbed in our activity, for example. But work is not play. It is good to play around at work once in a while. It lifts the spirits from the drudgery; but if you play too much, you accomplish nothing. It is partly right and partly wrong to say we should play at our work and work at our play.

We could describe the relation between play and competition, leisure and games in similar terms. Play is a narrower subset of exercise, leisure, competition, and games. The others are play if we do them for their pleasures. We engage in play for its own sake.

THE PARADOXES OF PLAY

Play can get complicated. In times past, short kids could play basketball and skinny kids could play football for hours on end because there was always a pickup game. Children now play fewer pickup sports than they once did because adult-sponsored leagues dominate children's sports. Children know the most important factor for a pickup ball game is fair teams. Neither stars nor bumblers relish a game where teams are stacked so that one side inevitably wins. Yet, in effect adults pick the sides in sports leagues, and the teams can be unfair enough to yield baseball scores of 18-1 and soccer scores of 10-0. So one result of sports organized by adults is that pleasure and play decline.[4] Referees and leagues coordinate, but also interfere with, play. Parents don't always like organized sports either, since they have to do endless driving. This is only one paradox of play. Others are:

To excel at games is more fun in the short run, but less in the end. If you excel, you taste the sweetness of accomplishment, of victory, of being "in the zone." But if you truly excel, you join a good team. Coaches of the better teams require practices early and late, in pouring rain and burning heat, to hone techniques and gain endurance. You battle through close games, where the tension is excruciating. For students, the bait is prestige and scholarships. For adults, a professional career in sports beckons. But there are always more athletes than openings.

Play is relaxing, but to relax too much spoils the fun. In athletics, there is no pleasure in scoring or winning when the opponent is unable to put up an effective defense. If you care about winning too much, it spoils the fun; but if you don't care enough, that ruins it too.

Play is liberation from the world of rules, but to play well, we need rules. Play has a certain openness and freedom, but if we play hide-and-seek or blindman's bluff, we spoil the game if we take a peek. A rule book cannot tell you how to play any sport; but without rules, competition is impossible. At the gym, one group may be goofing around and the other wants to start a game of basketball, until someone from the serious group says, "Quit playing around; we're trying to play basketball." The slackers are *playing*, but they aren't playing basketball.

Play is the opposite of work, but play can be very serious business. Among children, the boy or girl who decides what everyone plays is the class leader. Among adults, if an athlete gets paid $2 million per year, but one more injury could mean the end of his career, is he playing ball or working ball?

In a way, the very idea of reading, writing, and thinking hard about play seems a little strange. Do we need to *analyze* play? Thinking about play is not fun. Who wants to sit by a pile of books and read about play when it's sunny outside? If we craft a theology of play, will it make half the readers feel self-righteous and the other half feel guilty? For adults, half the joy of play is that we stop analyzing and do what comes naturally. Do we need to be told how to play? Didn't we master play as children and move on? Maybe we could say everything in twelve words: "Go out and play a while. It will be good for you." If only it were that simple. But sin and the Fall have tainted even play.

THE PERVERSION OF PLAY

Play certainly goes wrong, and thus it needs to be redeemed too. Some adults don't play enough. They are too alienated from their bodies to try athletic play. They work so hard and worry so much that spontaneity has drained from their lives. They feel guilty when they relax, so that they work hard even at their leisure. Some are too harried by social engagements to play. Others waste their leisure, leafing through newspapers and flipping through vapid television programs.

Some want to play all the time. Students fail in college due to their video game addictions. Adults lose jobs for playing games on their computers during work.

Some men play too hard. They have to win when they play, to prove themselves. A loss is a blow to their fragile ego. Losing makes them angry and sullen. They even cheat in order to win.

We can also play for the wrong reasons. People play to escape, to get away from work, to get away from home, to flee their meaningless lives. They live for the weekend. Play becomes an idol, as they find an identity in low golf scores or rock climbing skills.

Many men only play vicariously. They play through their children, dreaming that their child can achieve the athletic glory that eluded them. They compel their children to practice sports until the joy of childhood flees, or perhaps until they injure themselves.

Some only play through local teams. They feel that the star's touchdown or home run was theirs. Fanatical spectators can let passion for the achievements of a sports hero blind them to their own lack of accomplishment. They yearn to know ever more about their sports heroes but know ever less about themselves. Some men walk around mopey and sullen for days after someone on the local football team drops a pass at a critical moment. Their soul withers and dies (temporarily) because a teenager who attends the nearby university and suffers from an excess of human growth hormone misses a foul shot in the final seconds of a basketball game. Someone needs to shake these pitiable men and tell them the truth: "Those players don't know you. They don't care about you. If they did know you, they would not be your friend. They aren't from around here. They live here because someone offered them money to play here. Stop worrying about the speed and musculature of strangers. Wake up, get up, dust the potato chips off your expanding belly, go outside and put some fun into your own life."

Spectator sports have their defenders. They point out that sports teams foster community and let unexpressive men shout for joy and weep in sorrow.[5] But surely it is better to form community around relationships than around figures on a screen. Surely it is better to express our feelings daily, not just once a week during football season. Surely if we can choose between watching and playing, we should choose play.

The follies of play are numerous, but play can be immoral, not just foolish. Play goes astray when it indulges "the flesh" with licentiousness and carousing (Gal. 5:19-21). Play offends God when it includes obscene or coarse talk (Eph. 4:29; 5:4). Such jesting degrades everyone—the speaker, the hearer, and the object of the jokes. Play can be hedonistic and self-indulgent: "Eat, drink and be merry . . . for tomorrow we die" (Luke 12:19; 1 Cor. 15:32).

Ecclesiastes teaches that there is ultimately no pleasure when we live for nothing but the pleasures of laughter, wine, women, and song. "I refused my heart no pleasure. . . . Yet when I surveyed all that my hands had done . . . everything was meaningless, a chasing after the wind" (Eccl. 2:10-11). Amos says the quest for pleasure leads to boredom and a mindless search for distractions. In his day prosperous Israelites lapsed into "refined and sophisticated triviality" as they stretched out on couches, sang idle songs, and drank bowls of wine (Amos 6:4-6).[6]

Sports display the fallenness of play all too often. Excess competitiveness leads to hard fouls and flared tempers. The desire to win even leads athletes to cheat. For example, amateur tennis players must cover *their* side of the net when they call the lines and thus have to call their opponent's shots in or out. Honor requires players to call the lines honestly. But as my friends at Chesterfield Athletic Club will attest, sometimes the desire to win overwhelms a player. Once I played a very close doubles match with a league ranking on the line. After splitting the first two sets, my partner and I were playing very well in the decisive third set. But one player from the other team was keeping the match close by calling so many of our good shots "out" that even his partner yelled at him to quit cheating. Eventually we were ahead 5-3, with the cheater serving. My partner put away an overhead for our advantage. The cheater served to me with the match on the line. His serve came in hard but waist-high to my fore-hand and slightly wide. I swung hard but a little late, so that the ball rifled over the net, beyond the server's reach, near the line. We held our breath, then released it, as the ball landed inside the line by eight to twelve inches. We had won the match and headed toward the net for the traditional handshake. But after a long delay, the cheater called the ball out. Unable to stand another lie, I exploded "Out? That ball was in by a foot and you know it!" Guilty and dumbfounded, he replied, "Well, it might have been in by a few inches, but not a foot." He practically confessed, "I cheated, but not *that* much."

Why would anyone cheat while playing a *game*? Yet most men can remember a time when they cheated because somehow they felt they *had* to win. Sadly, we find more meaning in winning than in playing.

So we pervert play. But the perversions are not the essence of play. To base our attitude toward play on its abuses is like basing a book on humanity on visits to prisons. Everything God creates is good, but open to corruption. It is fallen, but not beyond redemption.

THE REDEMPTION OF PLAY

All men enjoy play, but believers should be most free to play, for three reasons. First, God the Creator has woven playfulness into His world. Second, God the Redeemer liberates us from burdens that impede play. Third, God the Provider permits play. Because God showers His grace on the evil and the good, everyone can play, but believers should be the first to play.

God's creation models playfulness. God may or may not play, but creation reveals His playfulness. Frolicking otters and puppies, col-orful salamanders and clown fish all display His exuberance and wit. The sheer diversity of colors, sounds, and smells shows God's play-fulness. Psalm 104:26 says God created leviathan to frolic in the sea. Wild animals play in the hills, declares Job 40:20.

After working six days, God rested for one, establishing our pat-tern for leisure and rest. By putting a boundary on work, He censured the urge to get and spend, get and spend. That permits us to sleep, play, and worship, to find contentment in what we have.[7]

The Gospels have no record of Jesus playing as a child.[8] Yet He shows His Father's commitment to rest rather than endless labor (Mark 6:30-32). Moreover, Jesus went to enough parties to be called "a glutton and a drunkard" (Matt. 11:19; Luke 7:34). We can even see playfulness in some of His teaching. In Matthew 23:24 He says the Pharisees, in their effort to keep their food pure, will "strain out a gnat but swallow a camel." The image is witty, but Jesus plays with sounds too. The original words were, "You strain out a *gamla* [gnat] but swallow a *kamla* [camel]."[9] It doesn't always translate well, but there is humor in the Bible.[10]

God's grace liberates play. Creation encourages honest play, and faith liberates it. Margaret Mead observed that "within traditional American culture . . . there runs a persistent belief that all leisure [and play] must be earned by work and good works." Further, while we can enjoy play and leisure, "it must be seen in a context of future work and good works."[11] But grace liberates us from the impulse to earn everything.

The redeemed man understands he cannot *earn* the right to rest. Indeed, the Gospel says we cannot truly *earn* anything. But when we trust in God, He gives us rest. He also gives us significance through our union with Him. Neither past nor future works can make us worthy of this. All is a gift of grace. Therefore we do not play "to justify our existence." Instead, when we play, we feel His pleasure.

Preparing to write this chapter, I read a small stack of books about play. Some theories were so sad and humorless that I wondered if the authors had ever played. Psychologists discussed play therapy for children; theologians wondered if play illumines the human condition; and philosophers ladled out Marxist analysis.

Play is the opiate of the masses, says the Marxist. Manipulative rulers promote sports heroes and rivalries so the proletariat forgets its oppression. They offer up violent spectacles, from gladiatorial shows to professional football, so the masses can burn off their aggression, misdirecting their rage onto referees or the captains of opposing teams. Play is an outlet for suppressed desires, says the Freudian. Alien moral codes can only control the dark impulses of mankind for so long. We occasionally need a burst of play, even revelry, like Mardi Gras. People need a dash of freedom so they can settle into their routine lives and work more effectively. Play is a distraction, says the existentialist. It diverts our attention, so we do not have to face the meaninglessness of life.[12]

The critics err when they make play so complicated and subversive. Yet they are not entirely wrong. Play *can* distract the lost from their seemingly insignificant existence. Men *do* use play as a potion to forget the misery and confinement of daily life. It *can* be a healthier form of the diversion others seek in alcohol or drugs.

But for the Christian man, play is celebration, not distraction. Of course, our lives can seem miserable and insignificant. But we do not deny our miseries. In the Gospel, we face our sin and inability and rejoice that God overcame them for us. We do not play after *we* work; we play after *God* works.

If so, then while the Lord's Day remains first a day of worship and rest, it also becomes a good day to play. I oppose Sunday leagues and tournaments that eliminate corporate worship and rest from our schedule, but I support casual play. When friends or family toss a Frisbee in the backyard, no one is demonstrating athletic prowess or competitive skills; they are just relaxing and celebrating life together. To play on Sunday is to play on the first day of the week. Most of America thinks we work five days, then rest and play on the weekend. But believers know we play *before* we work—on the first day of the week, not the week*end*. We do not earn our play with good works. Play, like rest, is a divine gift.

Furthermore, play, like rest, can turn our hearts toward Heaven. Its pleasures foreshadow "eternal pleasures" at God's right hand (Ps. 16:11). Its timelessness and its absence of hurrying hints at eternity. Our lack of skill can stir a yearning for perfection. Even the decline in our skills and the aches in our bones can teach us to long for the new creation.

God's grace liberates play, but with play, as in all of Christian living, there is still a place for law, *following* grace. Grace permits play, but without law, play is impossible. The prime law is love for our neighbor, respect for our partner in play. Because players have partners, we must exercise self-restraint. We refuse to play solely for self-gratification. For example, in a playful water fight, we forbid malice and bullying. The fastest person has to let the slowest person douse him too.

All play is rule-governed behavior. Sports need boundaries and procedures. Even make-believe has a kind of rule: The play has to strive to imitate reality. Even playing tea party, a child has the right to say, "No, that's not the way you do it."

God's providence permits play. Play is an activity born of abundance. When someone is starving or homeless, he can hardly play. We are free to play occasionally for the same reason that we rest weekly: We believe God will provide for us even if we do not guarantee every detail of life for ourselves. We can play freely when we feel confident that our basic needs will be met.

Perhaps that is why play is especially an activity of childhood. Children are free to play precisely because someone else is working, handing them food, clothing, shelter, and affection. Perhaps beloved children understand play better than adults because the flow of parental gifts has taught them they live by gifts, not by the sweat of their brow. Their parents' love has shown them providential grace. They know someone is working for their good, even when they are not. Therefore they can play.

After a death or a season of illness, depression, or unemployment, people need to rediscover play. Jesus told us we would face trouble, but He did not say we would experience unmitigated sorrow. Our Father gives good gifts to His children. Those who have suffered long need to break free from a mind-set of deprivation. We act on our trust in God when we play again.

PLAY THROUGH THE AGES

Reviewing my brief theology of play, I fear that some might accuse me of promoting Christian hedonism. The church's ancient wariness of pleasure surely devalues play. Augustine recognized that the normal desire to be happy and pain-free can cause men to live for pleasure. That, says Augustine, can lead them away from God, in whom they find real joy. Good things such as food, drink, music, art, and love become dangerous because our love of pleasure lets them control our soul, whether they lead to gluttony, drunkenness, and adultery or not.[13] For Augustine, conversion to Christianity meant conversion from hedonistic self-indulgence. He even questioned the mental pleasure of "vain" curiosity, the appetite to know something for its own sake. If every pleasure is dangerous, since it can lead us away from God and toward self-indulgence, then play is dangerous. According to Augustine, if play is simply delightful activity, it is suspect.

Many medieval theologians shared Augustine's concerns, but others supported festivals and celebrations. Calvin was an austere fellow, but he favored lawn bowling, even on Sundays. The Puritans have a reputation for despising sports, dancing, and other pleasures. Indeed, they did hold a strict view of the Sabbath, but they did not object to good food or beer any day, and they blessed chaste music and exercise the other six days a week.

Today everyone seems to love good times. And yet despite all the preachers who announce "God just wants you to be happy," many Christians are still distant heirs of Augustine. We like play and pleasure but feel uneasy about them. So we make pleasure a reward for hard work. Or we play for refreshment before the next onslaught of deadlines. We justify our sports as a way to stay fit or release tensions or make contacts or meet people. Must we always be goal-driven? Can't we say, "I just like to play"?

FIVE SUGGESTIONS TO IMPROVE OUR PLAY

Get out and play. Men in their thirties, forties, and fifties don't play as they once did. Bones ache, and schedules tighten. We arrive home late and weary. We slump onto the sofa with a newspaper in one hand and a clicker in the other, watching news or sports and reading the paper during commercials. Resist, my brothers. Years ago I made a commitment. If I have a choice between playing and watching others play, I will play—every time. I will not watch sports on television if I can get up, get out, and play. Will you join me?

Lighten up. Even if we do stick with sports, our ability to enjoy them often declines. Further, men who excel at a sport are too cool to say so. Stars at golf and tennis concede, "I play a little." At most they offer the nonchalant oxymoron, "I'm a serious player." What is a "serious player"? Does it mean fifty-dollar lessons? Hours watching the golf channel? Vacations planned around the sport of choice?

The older we get, the more solemn our play becomes. As they grew up, my children used to play restaurant. They crafted colorful menus with huge decorations but few items:

Crakers $2.00
Steak $3.00
Soup $2.50

The waitress (me) always had an accent from Germany or Scotland. After initial politeness to the customers (who had names like Gortha Flinderpotts and Sicily Syzygy), she got bossy: "What will you have, dearies? Come on. Hurry up. I can't wait here all day while you decide if you want broccoli or cauliflower! There are only two choices, so *pick* one. Yes, yes, that's lovely." But things slowly became more authentic. The prices became accurate, the menu realistic. Today my eleven-year-old daughter and her friend have a "pretend" design studio and mail-order catalog center with such accurate drawings and prices that I think they will look at each other soon and say, "Why *play* at this? Let's start our own business." All they need is a slightly naive venture capitalist.

My daughter is now exiting the world of fantasy that most men abandoned long ago. We don't play store—we *run* the store. As we get older, even our play becomes like work. We pressure ourselves for results, such as weight loss or improved skills. If we really play, we reenter a world where it's safe to make mistakes. We don't have to achieve or prove anything. When we work, we must fulfill our duties and accomplish our tasks whether we like it or not. But play-ers are free agents. Players don't force themselves to submit to gru-eling workouts. If we sweat, it's because we love the game too much to play halfheartedly.

Enjoy yourself. Play means skipping instead of walking, bounc-ing instead of standing still. Players don't put their shoes away; they try to throw them up the steps, over the staircase, and into their bed-room—and they shout for joy if they succeed.

It's hard to sing or play when we are sad. The Israelites could not sing a song of Zion when they lived in Babylon (Ps. 137:1-4). But when they returned to their land, their "mouths were filled with laughter" and their "tongues with songs of joy" (Ps. 126:1-2). The Lord puts songs in our hearts and voices. He richly gives us all things for our enjoyment (1 Tim. 6:17-19).

Augustine and Aquinas thought Christians should never do anything—eat or kiss or play music—for pleasure, since pleasure encourages the lusts of the flesh. They were wrong. The Song of Solomon praises romantic love. Ecclesiastes says it is a gift of God to find pleasure in food and drink (2:24-25; 3:12-14). Paul says every-thing is good if "consecrated by the word of God and prayer" (1 Tim. 4:4-5). "When God gives any man wealth and possessions, and enables him to enjoy them, to accept his lot and be happy in his work—this is a gift of God" (Eccl. 5:19).

Christians do not *live* for pleasure (Prov. 21:17; 1 Tim. 5:6), but pleasure is not evil either. Moses commanded Israel to use part of the tithes for the poor and for priests, but part for a feast in God's tem-ple. "Buy whatever you like: cattle, sheep, wine or other fermented drink, or anything you wish. Then you and your household shall eat there in the presence of the LORD your God and rejoice" (Deut. 14:22-29, v. 26 quoted; cf. Ps. 104:15). We have gone far wrong when teenagers sign up for school sports less to play the game than to build a résumé for college applications.

Get involved, body and mind. Card games and board games like chess are mostly mental, but ideally play engages both mind and body. This is most obvious when we play music or play charades. But for the millions whose main physical exertion at work involves tapping a keyboard, play often creates a blessed reunion with their bodies. Sadly, we can become estranged from our bodies, especially as we age. They hurt in strange places; they get lumpy and gray. They bungle familiar tasks and forget old skills. When we play, we call our bodies back into active service. If we play enough, dormant talents return. At best, play absorbs the whole man, from balding head to aching heels. Players leave ordinary space and sail into another world.

If you can't play, at least be playful. A few men retire at fifty-two to perfect their golf game, but for the rest of us, the older we get, the less we play. Yet, as life becomes more complicated, as responsibilities and burdens add up, we need to play as much as ever. Part of the cure is fostering a playful spirit. Let me illustrate:

- If the music your child is playing sounds like a chain saw buzzing through a roll of barbed wire, don't shout, "Turn off that hideous noise." Walk into her room and wink cheerfully. "Could you turn that up a little? It's my favorite song this week."
- Professional athletes work hard at their game, risking health, reputation, and income every day. Despite the risk, some insert a "love of the game" clause in their contract, saying they can play their game anytime, anywhere, with any result without breaching the contract.
- Preachers have the sober responsibility of pointing out the sins and follies of mankind. But they can denounce and condemn them from the pulpit's heights, or they can step down to laugh at themselves once in a while. Both lines of action can foster repentance.
- Playfulness means taking responsibility to have fun. People can be both playful and productive—perhaps *more* productive—at work.[14]

A few days ago I sat with a group in the bleachers at a rather boring baseball game. When a couple of women went to the concession stand and asked us to watch their seats, they disappeared so long that we began to ignore the game and joke about why they were gone so long:

"Maybe they wanted prime rib instead of a hot dog—that would take longer to cook."

"Maybe they wanted wine instead of a beer. They would have to send out for that."

"Maybe they wanted something that's really hard to get at a concession stand—an apology."

The last line is a play on the word *concession* that eventually led to a cartoon listing the prices of varying apologies.

> I take your point $1.50
> I have to admit I was wrong $2.50
> It was all my fault $3.25
> All right, all right, you win $4.00

CONCLUSION

Play is like a greasy pig—slippery but fun. Play is hard to analyze because it is both an action and an attitude. Two athletes can run side by side, yet one is playing, the other toiling. Two lecturers can speak a room apart. One wields his dullness like a weapon, bludgeoning his stupefied audience to sleep. The other uses wit and imagination to engage his partners in a dance through his topic, so that an hour seems to last five minutes.

Playfulness is a way of life. It means not taking everything too seriously, not acting as if everything rides on us. For the best players, levity is never escape, never denial. The best players know who they are—sons of a playful God. The redeemed play without guilt because they know they do not need to justify their existence by their good works. We know our heavenly Father will provide for us; so we can play, at least occasionally, like His little children.

DISCUSSION QUESTIONS

1. How often do you play? If you don't play enough, are the obstacles external (e.g., your schedule) or internal (e.g., loss of a playful heart)? How can you restore and refresh play in your life?

2. Do you prefer to play or to watch others play? Explain and evaluate your answer.
3. Why do many men feel they must win when they play? What would you say to such a man?
4. Why do we play? Do you see play as a diversion? A reward for hard work? A reflection of God's nature? A divine gift? Does your view of play affect the way you play?

11

THE GLORY AND THE MISERY
OF MAN

In the 2000 Olympics, Sammy Henson ended a storied wrestling career by winning the silver medal in a hard-fought contest. But Henson took no pleasure in second place. When the match ended, he sprinted off the mat and emitted a primal scream of anguish. He fell to the floor, kicking and wailing. At the medal ceremony, he wept openly, then hurled his silver medal to the ground. Since childhood, Henson had dreamed of the glory of gold; anything less was misery.

The hunger for excellence, even glory, rests deep in our hearts. Some yearn for championships. But even if we don't seek the top rank, we expect the best of ourselves. Musicians count on playing the right notes, with expressive phrasing. Speakers expect to master their content and win their audience to it. Athletes view their best days as normal. After excelling, performers don't marvel at their incredible luck. They say, "That's the way it's supposed to be" and begin planning to do even better the next time. Similarly, though managers and administrators know large projects never go smoothly, glitches still feel odd. Craftsmen expect to do the right thing the right way the first time. Even repairmen half-anticipate fixing things promptly and permanently. When they cannot induce pipes, wires, or computer programs to run properly, they are as likely to say, "That's odd" as to say, "That's typical." Through it all, excellence seems normal, and failure seems jarring.

The drive to excel testifies that God designed us for glory. He created us in His image, as the crown of creation. He designed humanity to govern the world for Him. He charged us to be fruitful and multiply, to rule the earth and subdue it. He commissioned us to represent His rule, so that all things are subject to Him through us (Gen. 1—2).

Children's books like to say every little girl is a princess, but they are too modest. Mankind is a race of kings and queens, overseeing the earth on God's behalf. In all things God charges us to rule for Him—at work, at home, and at play. When we pull weeds and plant seeds, we develop creation's potential for beauty and fruit. As we govern our homes and schedules, as we develop mind and body, we become instruments honed for God's use.

Perhaps this sounds grandiose. Govern the world for God? I can hardly govern my desktop. Subdue the earth? I can hardly subdue the crabgrass in my yard. When a lawn care analyst accosts me with the ugly truth about my grass-to-weed ratio, I may say, "They may seem like weeds to you, but actually, I'm fostering biodiversity," but the ugly truth remains. In some moods, we love ironic sayings like, "Experience is a great teacher. It allows you to recognize a mistake when you do it the second time."

Self-government is even more elusive. How shall we make our minds instruments of God's rule? Do we acquire a taste for heavy reading as we do for gourmet coffee, a sip at a time? Can we make our bodies God's instruments if pushing aside chips and dips is a challenge? God knows the apparent absurdity of it all and addresses it in Hebrews.

JESUS AND OUR ASPIRATIONS

Hebrews provides us with a proper self-understanding. But it does not begin, as many books do, by assuring us of our supreme worth. Indeed, Hebrews does not begin with mankind at all. Rather, it directs our attention to Jesus—the Son of God, the radiance of His glory, the Creator and sustainer of creation, the Savior who provided purification for sins (1:1-3). He sits at God's right hand, ruling from His throne, until all His enemies are subject to Him (1:8-13). Hebrews only turns to mankind in 2:5-15, where we hear high praise from Psalm 8:[1]

> *What is man that you are mindful of him, the son of man that you care for him? You made him a little lower than the heavenly beings and crowned him with glory and honor. You made him ruler over the works of your hands; you put everything under his feet.*
>
> —vv. 4-6

This sort of acclaim certainly boosts our self-esteem. But as we read on, the description of human majesty in Hebrews begins to sound a little *too* lofty: "In putting everything under him, God left nothing that is not subject to him" (2:8). The statement that *everything* is subject and *nothing* is not subject clashes with our experience. But Hebrews immediately adds: "Yet at present we do not *see* everything subject to him. But we do see Jesus, who was made a little lower than the angels, now crowned with glory and honor . . ." (emphasis added).

So Hebrews does agree with our experience. Indeed, the physical environment and human society are in such disarray that the call to rule the world seems a joke. We can hardly govern ourselves, let alone the world. But, Hebrews adds, we *do* see Jesus (2:9). Everything *is* under *His* feet. He *is* crowned with glory and honor; He fulfills God's goal for mankind.

The praise of mankind is *most* true of Jesus, the One True Man. He was lower than the angels for a little while. Yet He is now crowned with glory and honor and rules over all things. After the Fall, Psalm 8 primarily describes Jesus, but it also depicts our union with Him, our representative. Jesus fulfilled the charge God gave us—to rule. Then He took us with Him to the glory God planned for us. As Hebrews 2:9-10 puts it:

*Jesus . . . [is] now crowned with glory and honor because he suf-
fered death, so that by the grace of God he might taste death for
everyone. In bringing many sons to glory, it was fitting that God,
for whom and through whom everything exists, should make the
author of their salvation perfect through suffering.*

God created mankind in His image and crowned us with glory. By
rebelling, we ruined that glory. But Jesus redeemed us from our ruin,
and so God crowned Him with glory and honor. He could have kept
the glory scheduled for us to Himself. But "he [is] bringing many sons
to glory." That is, *He wants us to share His glory.* Therefore, He endured
a humiliation greater than ours, in order to bring us a joy that is near
to His: "By the grace of God, he . . . taste[d] death for everyone."

To "taste death" means to experience death. On the cross, *He*
experienced the consequences of *our* rebellion, that we might live
with Him and that He might bring us to glory (2:10). Jesus removed
both our subjective feeling of misery over our abominable behavior
and the objective fact of our fallenness before God. He felt compassion for our misery and acted to remove it.

Hebrews says it is "fitting" for Jesus to rescue us (2:10) because
God is gracious, loving, and good. It fits God's character to do this
through Jesus, the "author" of salvation. The word "author" is
unusual. The original is a compound word whose parts mean "chief"
and "leader." Jesus is our chief leader, our pioneer, trailblazer, hero,
or champion. In context, "champion" is a good translation because
Jesus fought and defeated our great foe, Satan. He is also a "trailblazer" because we follow His path.

JESUS, CHAMPION OF MANKIND

We rarely think of Jesus as our champion, but the idea is biblical. In
antiquity, some battles were settled when two champions engaged in
combat on behalf of their people. For example, David and Goliath
fought each other as champions of their armies. The troops were at
a standoff; so they resolved the impasse by letting the two champions represent them (1 Sam. 17).

The idea of champions fighting on behalf of their people is also modern. In elections, political parties put forward their champions and whoever wins, wins for the whole party. In athletic championships, teams represent their school, city, or state. If a city's team wins, the whole city feels it has won too.

All of us have cheered for a champion who represents us, even though the applause can sound faintly ridiculous. We hold our nose and vote for politicians with glaring flaws. We cheer for athletes who play for our team solely because the local billionaire owner won a bidding war for the star's talents.

But Jesus is one champion who deserves our cheers. He calls Himself our champion, a hero who defeats our malevolent foe. Jesus compares Satan to "a strong man, fully armed" who "guards his own house." But Jesus is stronger: "When someone stronger attacks and overpowers him, he takes away the armor in which the man trusted and divides up the spoils" (Luke 11:21-22). Jesus "bind[s] the strong man" (Matt. 12:29; Mark 3:27, KJV) by casting out demons, healing disease, and proclaiming God's reign. But above all, he "shared in their humanity so that by his death he might destroy . . . the devil—and free those who all their lives were held in slavery by their fear of death" (Heb. 2:14-15).

Jesus is the victor, but, paradoxically, He won by appearing to lose. He achieved victory over Satan by letting Satan's minions kill Him, then rising from death. By coming to "taste death" (Heb. 2:9) *for* us, He broke Satan's quasi-legitimate hold *over* us. Satan's hold is quasi-legitimate because he can truly say we are wicked and deserve to die (Rev. 12:10). But when Jesus died in our place, Satan lost the right to accuse us. By rising, Jesus also liberated us from the fear of death. He demonstrated that resurrection, not death, is the final word.

JESUS' ACCEPTANCE OF US

So Jesus is our champion. Unlike many heroes, however, He never despises or looks condescendingly upon His admirers. He is not like an entertainer who tries to escape adoring mobs but like a politician who wades into the crowds (though for more noble purposes). But Jesus does not make contact because of an impending election (kings are not reelected). He seeks us because He loves us and is proud of us. Hebrews says, "Jesus is not ashamed to call them brothers" (2:11).

Of course, he *could* be ashamed of us. Almost every clan has a shameful relative, an uncle perhaps with no social grace, no job, missing teeth, and perhaps an indictment or two. In God's family, you and I are prime candidates to embarrass God our Father. We do plenty that might shame our older brother, Jesus. Yet, amazingly, He is not ashamed to call us brothers, nor is the Father "ashamed to be called [our] God" (11:16).

Let me put it differently. I hesitate to put Christian bumper stickers on my car because I wonder if my driving is up to it. I'm not a reckless driver, but I don't want Jesus' reputation to be identified with every hurried decision I make on the road. I might shame Him. But my hesitation is trifling, since my life as a whole is much like a car adorned with Christian stickers. You and I commit crimes, misdemeanors, and follies that could dishonor Jesus. These acts render us unworthy of being part of Jesus' family. Nonetheless, God loves us and claims us as His children.

Many men long for this pure acceptance and seek it in vain from their fathers.

• Our fathers said, "You will never amount to anything; you will never do anything right." But God declares, "These are the good works I prepared for you to do" (see Eph. 2:10).

• Our fathers said, "You weakling." But Jesus whispers, "I empathize with your weakness."

• Our parents hissed, "You should be ashamed of yourself." But Jesus call us His brothers and shares His glory with us. Paul exults, "And we, who with unveiled faces all reflect the Lord's glory, are being transformed into his likeness with ever-increasing glory" (2 Cor. 3:18).

Jesus is like a man proudly introducing two of His beloved friends to each other. He presents God the Father to us and presents us to the Father. He declares the Father's excellence to us: "In the presence of the congregation I will sing your praises" (Heb. 2:12). But he also presents us, His brothers, to God: "Here am I, and the children God has given me" (v. 13).

How amazing, how liberating! There is, deep within every man, a feeling that he must prove himself. Of course, many give up and decide to do barely enough to get by. Still, most men want to prove themselves by performing notable deeds. Yet we all have multiple flaws; so we doubt that we have proven ourselves. Whatever we achieve, it is never enough. And even if we become number one, we have to stay there, which is another uncertain proposition. Jesus bids us to quit the performance game. He accepts us as family, just as we are.

Of course, struggles continue even after God accepts us. If Jesus, our big brother, "taste[d] death" though crowned with glory and honor, we ought to expect adversity too. God announced His pleasure with Jesus from the beginning, but there is a sense in which He also brought Jesus to completion through suffering (Heb. 2:10). Jesus is our elder brother, and we younger brothers should expect our lives to echo His, in suffering and in glory (Heb. 2:11-13; 1 Pet. 1:11; 4:13-14; 5:1).

JESUS AND OUR FAILURE

We now have the elements for a sober self-concept: We enjoyed grandeur at creation; we fell into misery through sin. Then we returned to grandeur in Christ. The grandeur-misery-grandeur pattern is our condition. A realistic self-concept makes us expect to succeed, but also to fail and to feel miserable over it. The thought, *I should be doing better* is fundamentally true. We belong to a great family, a family of champions. God made us for something better than failure, whether *failure* means sin or poor performance. Since we belong to God's excellent family, we can handle disappointment. But first, recall some fruitless strategies we use to manage failure:

- We indulge in self pity: "I'm a wretched, miserable failure. No one is worse than me."
- We wallow in self-recrimination: "I failed myself; I failed those who love and trust me. People should stay away from me, and I wish I could get away from myself."
- We shift blame and get angry at others: "I failed, but it's really *his* fault."
- We resolve with grim determination to do better next time—and forever: "I'll never commit *that* mistake again."
- We brush it off, pretending we did not fail or do not care. Or, like the fans who once attended games of the New Orleans Saints with bags over their heads, we create ironic detachment from ourselves. We berate ourselves, calling ourselves idiots or dummies and cursing ourselves.

But because we possess a secure identity in Christ, knowing that God loves and accepts us despite our blunders, we have better ways to respond to failure:

- If we do our best, but our performance falls short, we can accept that, saying, "I did my best, but it was not God's will to bless my labors just now."
- If we sin, we count reproof as a blessing (Prov. 9:9). We say, "I failed because I erred" or "I failed because I was not diligent." We ask for mercy and hope to learn a lesson, but we know better than to vow "never again." We probably *will* do it again—and there will be mercy on that day too.
- If we cannot detect why we faltered, other options remain. If we "fail" in a good cause, we can view it as experimental scientists do. Edison tried hundreds of substances before finding one that worked as the glowing filament for his light bulb. But for Edison, the flameouts were not failures, they were minor successes. Each one taught him one more way *not* to do it. Above all, let us recall that God loves us and calls us His own, however we may fail.

If we know who we are, it is easier to accept disappointments. I think of the American poet Billy Collins, whose brilliant, witty word pictures will never succeed, if *success* means winning a mass audience, because *there is no mass audience* for poetry in America. I think of Kierkegaard, his writings neglected for a century, and recall a Christian bookseller commenting acidly on a new monograph, "It will never sell; it's too good." But what if God calls you to write poetry? What if you are a musician who fits no marketing niche? Or an inventor who is too far ahead of the times? Know this: Human taste is fallible. God prizes faithfulness, not success. If we please Him, believing *His* appraisal matters most, we can "fail" without fear.

For example, I am part of a group that is launching an institute to broker quality ideas by less-known Christian thinkers. The cause is good, but it may "fail" from lack of funding and workers. We could avoid the pain of defeat by doing nothing. Instead, we will do our best in the allotted time and will pray for blessing. If it is a "minor success," may God raise others to do it better.

HEROISM TODAY

I believe Christian men can secure their identity, in part, by knowing Jesus as the hero who accepts us. But this idea is hard to grasp because our culture has lost its sense of the heroic. Materialism reduces mankind to "an accidental collocation of atoms." How can an arrangement of atoms be "heroic"? Classical psychology explains great achievements as the expression of suppressed desires. Freud reduced the heroic accomplishments of Leonardo da Vinci to the outworking of a sublimated homosexuality. Behaviorism and economic materialism claim that every human action seeks a reward. All behavior, they assume, attempts to meet a need or desire. Therefore, they allege, Mother Theresa did not give herself to the poorest of India because she *cared* about them. She did it to meet her ego needs—perhaps to prove her worth or make a name for herself. Economists observe that every good deed can reap a reward and propose that everyone is so motivated. In these ways, every sacrifice is explained away. Cynicism rules.

Of course, we still have heroes, but they are one-dimensional.

Athletes are mighty men of the slam dunk, the sixty-yard touch-down pass, or the home run blast. Rock stars play blistering guitars, and opera divas have three-octave ranges. Actors' perfectly sculpted faces mimic every human emotion on camera. Once the media bestows celebrity status on such celebrities, children can hang their posters on the wall, and adults can read their intimate interviews.[2]

But don't look too closely at their personal lives. After they throw, swing, sing, or act, they have less ideas about the good life than you do. Charles Barkley, the former all-star NBA forward and barroom brawler, used his verbal skills to entertain sportswriters after games and to enrage foes during them. Asked about his chaotic personal life one day, Barkley thundered the awful truth, "I am not a role model."

But the loss of role models cannot occur without lament. We need to recapture our sense of the heroic, because role models can outline the good life. We need true heroes.

One of my heroes is a retired college professor named Willard McMillan. Willard was sixty-two when I joined his Bible department at Geneva College in 1986. At 5'10" and 135 pounds, with a bald pate, a raspy voice, and imperfect posture, his physical persona is unimpressive. But Willard is my hero. Hard-working and intelligent, he is a captivating speaker and a witty conversationalist. Endlessly cheerful, he welcomes everyone who crosses his path. In meetings, Willard speaks sparingly but with such timing, gravity, and zeal for truth that his minimal words have maximal effect. Willard and I taught required Bible survey classes together. With 300 students, some inevitably were displeased with their grades. When they complained to me, my insecurity as a new professor sometimes led to defensiveness. Not Willard. However students grumbled when they *entered* his office, they always smiled as they *exited*. I eavesdropped to discover his secret: He let them talk themselves out, then equipped them to grade themselves, then suggested methods to improve. This became one of many "wisdom of Willard" proverbs I learned as I watched him live out his insights.

HEROISM AND CHRISTIAN LIVING

My initial impulse to imitate Willard was instinctive. Later I realized that the New Testament often commands us to imitate the wise and godly. About twelve times the Bible invites us to imitate God (e.g., Eph. 4:32; 5:1). More frequently, Scripture bids us to imitate an apostle or another leader (e.g., Phil. 4:9; 2 Thess. 3:7-9; Heb. 13:7). Both commands astonish me. It would approach blasphemy for puny men to dare to imitate God if He did not solicit it. And it would approach folly for one sinful man to imitate another if God did not command it.

Why, then, does God command it? Because humans are imitators. When John says, "Do not imitate what is evil but what is good," he *assumes* we will imitate someone (3 John 11). Some want to imitate rebellion and vice. Others strive to imitate God. Still others follow the wise, who display their insight by their excellent life (Jas. 3:13).

Heroes *model* greatness. Their example supplies a vision of maturity that captures our imagination and inspires us. We think, "I want to be like that." We need models of excellence because many Christians think rule-keeping is the essence of Christianity.

A few years ago I met with a group of twenty-five leading Christian youths, aged sixteen to twenty, from an excellent church. I asked them, "How many of you would say the *essence* of your Christian life is this: First, you don't do certain things other kids your age do, like drinking alcohol, smoking cigarettes or marijuana, or experimenting sexually. Second, you do some things they don't— you go to church, read the Bible, and seek Christian friends. Raise your hand if you think these two things are the essence of your faith." All but one raised a hand. *Their doing was the core of their faith.*

Perhaps young Christians are especially susceptible to such thinking. But adults can succumb to soft legalism too (see Chapter 1). We think, "If I just do these things, I will please God." But the essence of Christian living is knowing God, trusting Him, and conforming to Him, not rule-keeping.[3] Christian conduct flows from who we *are*. When God renews our mind and spirit, we do good deeds spontaneously and naturally, just as healthy apple trees naturally bear apples. We cannot change ourselves by resolving to keep external regulations.

God delivers us from legalism, but we also avoid legalism by finding heroes and accepting them as models. Good models inspire us. They give us a vision of a godly life and help us live by patterns of godliness, not just legal codes. Sometimes heroic believers who have gone before us supply the models (Heb. 11). But Jesus is the best pattern we could imitate. He teaches morals, but His life offers a model of excellence that captures the imagination. He makes us say, "I want to be like that."

Think, for example, of Jesus' relational style. He moved in every circle, dining with aristocrats and fishermen, with Pharisees and tax-collectors. He engaged Jews, Gentiles, and Samaritans in conversation. He ministered in city and countryside, with disciples and opponents. He treated all with dignity; yet if someone had a faulty agenda, he shifted it. If someone asked an unhelpful question, he modified it so He could answer what they should have asked. He feared nothing—not rejection, not death, not contamination by contact with unholy people. He knew they would catch His purity long before He caught their pollution.

Jesus is our hero because he *shares* our humanity, yet *surpasses* it. In times of trouble, we may say, "Misery loves company." Yes, but it is more true to say, "Misery loves relief." Jesus provides relief. He shares our weaknesses in order to lead us out of them. He is our hero, yet He humbled Himself; so He can empathize with us. He knows our weaknesses and still loves us. Our empathetic hero invites us to a heroic life like His own.

THE ABSENCE OF HEROISM: OUR SHAME AND JESUS' CURE

We often misconstrue Paul's famous statement, "All have sinned and fall short of the glory of God" (Rom. 3:23). We tend to think Paul says the same thing twice—we are sinners, sinners! But Paul makes two distinct points. First, *we sin*. That is, we violate God's Law and transgress His standards and so become guilty. Second, *we fall short of glory*. That is, we lack greatness. We fail to reflect the divine majesty, as Adam and Eve once did, and so we are ashamed of ourselves.

Jesus solves the problem of sin, which creates guilt and lack of glory, which in turn creates shame. First, He cures our guilt by atoning for our sins. He kept the Law for us and gave His righteousness to us. Thus, when we stand before God, the Judge, He will declare us "not guilty." Jesus' atonement grants us good legal standing with God (see Rom. 3:21—5:21). We are justified or declared righteous. Second, Jesus cures our shame by adopting us and assuring us of His love (Rom. 8:12-39).

Shame is a complicated phenomenon. People ought to be ashamed of some things, such as sin. Indeed, to have no shame is to be oblivious to God's standards. Shamelessness is a sign of a defective conscience (Jer. 6:15; 8:12).[4] On the other hand, we can become ashamed when there is no guilt. If our body is too large or too small, too lean or too fleshy, we can be ashamed of it. Facial blemishes, hair loss, and a weak voice can all induce feelings of shame. If we have less money than our peers, if our clothes or cars fall short of social norms, we can feel ashamed. If we lack a skill, if we are clumsy or computer illiterate or hesitant in speech, we may be ashamed. A chart may clarify the idea.

Moral sphere: *Our doing*	Personal sphere: *Our being*
Keep rules –> *Righteousness*	Display greatness –> *Glory*
Break rules –> *Sin, guilt*	Display deviance –> *Shame*
Solution for guilt: *Atonement*	Solution for shame: *Acceptance, achievement*

Everyone seems to neglect one element of the guilt-shame duo. Contemporary pagans deny the existence of a transcendent, moral God. If there is no God, there are no absolute moral standards, and hence there is no objective guilt. People *feel* guilty for falling short of local standards, but friends and therapists can help them overcome their feelings. Christians, meanwhile, focus on guilt and neglect shame, except as a feeling that follows any exposure of misdeeds. But guilt and shame are both valid categories.[5] We can describe their relationship this way:

THE EXPERIENCE OF CHRISTIANS
(ROMANS 3:23)

Break rules -> *Guilt* -> (partial overlap with) *shame*

Lack glory -> *Shame* -> (partial overlap with) *guilt*

We know Jesus removes our guilt, but He also erases our shame and starts us toward glory.

• First, if we are ashamed due to guilt, our guilt must be covered or removed. Jesus removed our guilt by coming to "taste death" in our place (Heb. 2:9).

• Second, our shame dissolves if we know we are beloved and accepted despite our failures. Jesus loves and accepts us. He is proud that we joined His family. Though we do much that might embarrass Him, "he is not ashamed to call [us] brothers" (Heb. 2:11).

• Third, we overcome shame if we do something great or significant. If an athlete's mistake costs his team a victory, he feels ashamed; but if his stellar performance wins the next two games, he is exonerated. Likewise, after Jesus covers our guilt, He empowers us to do notable deeds. We perform the good works He prepared for us. We begin to undo the effects of the curse. We *can* govern the earth for God.

THE QUEST FOR EXCELLENCE REVISITED

It is good to know that Jesus forgives and accepts us. Important practical implications follow:

Understand your desire to excel. There is nothing wrong with a passion to excel. It is right to apply our God-given energies to make the most of our abilities. The desire for excellence is natural, and it is honest to admit that.[6] Sammy Henson reminds us that we are bound for anguish if our *identity* depends on our performance. But God designed us to reflect His glory. We have lost much of it, but it is proper to seek its restoration.

Help others excel. There is nothing wrong with aspiring for greatness, but to attain glory by squashing, dominating, or ignoring others is another matter. God created *mankind* for glory. Therefore, godly men yearn to take others with them to restored grandeur. We instinctively nurture and develop the potential of our children. But we can neglect our wives, though God destined them for glory too. So let us sacrifice some of our development to foster theirs. "Every marriage moves either towards enhancing one another's glory or toward degrading each other." We should draw our wives toward their glory, and let them do the same for us.[7]

We should enlist members of our community to remove the curse and to seek God-pleasing glory. People set their sights too low. "I hope to make it to the weekend," they sigh. "I'm a survivor," they boast. A plague on such pitifully small goals! Let us aspire for grandeur together.

Let your excellence enlighten others. Like it or not, every decent man is someone's hero, someone's refuge from the storm (Isa. 32:1-4). Fathers are heroes to sons and daughters. Teachers and leaders set standards. Therefore guard yourselves, for people *do* imitate you. The way you treat your body and your friends, the way you control or indulge your emotions, words, and calendar—it all functions as someone's model.

CONCLUSION

We aspire to grandeur because God designed mankind to partake of His glory and to govern creation for Him. But we rebelled and lost both our grandeur and our sense of direction. We sin and feel guilty; we fail and feel ashamed. We retain some glory; yet it hurts to know God purposed more for us. Jesus cures us. He removes our guilt and restores our honor. He accepts us into His family. He reinstates our rank and strength. He resets our moral compass. His life models the greatness we seek. Our Lord has rescued us from our misery and restored us to glory. Let us live like it.

DISCUSSION QUESTIONS

1. How large is the gap between your aspirations to glory and your achievements? How painful is the gap? Restate this chapter's answer to your misery.
2. How do you handle failure? How would your response to failure change if you could fully rest in the providence and loving acceptance of God?
3. Describe one or two of your chief heroes. What have you learned from them?
4. Do you think of Jesus as your hero? What could you gain from meditating on His life pattern?
5. How is your conscience functioning? Does it rightly lead you through the shame-guilt maze?

Epilogue

Someone once said, "No one ever finishes a book—they just stop writing." Just so, I now stop, though unfinished business remains. I see questions left unanswered: Does virtue have a gender? Is the godliness of men different from the godliness of women (Does 90 percent of this book hold for women too?) What are the other principles for discipline, after "proportional justice" and "quantity time yields quality time"? Then there are questions about the way our culture affects our efforts to live biblically. How can men be rich toward God when the culture urges us to plow all excess into investment plans and retirement savings? What are the effects of working in a market economy where people will sell *anything*—silk, marble, spices, wine, cattle, even the "bodies and souls of men" (Rev 18:11-13)? Don't we make and sell things, to this day, that harm both the buyer and the seller, just because there is a profit in it?

But I don't fret over the unfinished business. Other teachers and authors can address them. Much more, my confidence rests in God's work in you, by both the external means of Scripture and the internal means of His Spirit. Because I believe in the power of the Word, I spent more time on Bible exposition than most books of this type: for companionship, Genesis 2; for romance, Proverbs 5; for fatherhood, Exodus 34; for friendship, Ecclesiastes 4; for leadership, 1 Timothy 3; for money, Luke 12 and Matthew 6; for identity, Hebrews 2. I hope my words faithfully explored the Word.

Still more important is God's secret work in the hearts of men. He enlightens us and draws us to Himself. The last chapter argued that noble heroes can capture the imagination and can effect positive change. The Lord Himself is the godly man's ultimate hero, of course. As we love Him and behold Him, we will grow into His likeness, as He has promised.

This thought leads to the core of all that this book has explored. As I close, I want to rehearse again the roots of godly manhood. The first root is the knowledge that no man becomes good 1) by resolving to change or 2) by adopting multi-step plans for success in marriage, parenting, work, and play. The second root is the knowledge that God Himself is the source and the paradigm of godly manhood. Godly husbands love their wives as Christ loves the church. Godly fathers act like the heavenly Father, echoing His love, justice, faithfulness, and discipline. Godly friends act as God has acted, showing self-disclosure and helpful presence, the twin marks of friendship. Godly workers love to create because the Creator God made us in His image. When we finish our tasks, we resemble Jesus who exulted, "It is finished." Even in play, we imitate the playful deeds and words of God. He organized time to promote rest and play among His children, who know how to stop working and to rest in Him.

May it be so for us. Let us rest first in the work of Christ our Savior, who has reconciled us to Himself, whatever our failures and demerits. Then let us rest in Him. As we behold His face, may we be transformed into His likeness and glory, into men with a heart for God.

Recommended Reading

The Gospel and Christian Living

Jerry Bridges, *Transforming Grace* (Colorado Springs: NavPress, 1991).

Bryan Chapell, *Holiness by Grace* (Wheaton, IL: Crossway Books, 2001).

Daniel Doriani, *Putting the Truth to Work* (Phillipsburg, NJ: P & R, 2001) (for pastors).

John Piper, *Future Grace* (Sisters, OR: Multnomah, 1998).

Christopher Wright, *Walking in the Ways of the Lord* (Downers Grove, IL: InterVarsity Press, 1995).

Manhood

Jack Balswick, *Men at the Crossroads* (Downers Grove, IL: InterVarsity Press, 1992).

David Brooks, *Bobos in Paradise: The New Upper Class and How They Got There* (New York: Simon & Schuster, 2000).

R. Kent Hughes, *Disciplines of a Godly Man* (Wheaton, IL: Crossway Books, 1991).

Dick Keyes, *True Heroism in a World of Celebrity Counterfeits* (Colorado Springs: NavPress, 1995).

Patrick Morley, *The Man in the Mirror* (Nashville: Thomas Nelson, 1992).

David Wells, *Losing our Virtue: Why the Church Must Recover Its Moral Vision* (Grand Rapids, MI: Eerdmans, 1998).

Marriage and Family

Rodney Clapp, *Families at the Crossroads: Beyond Traditional & Modern Options* (Downers Grove, IL: InterVarsity Press, 1993).

James Olthius, *I Pledge You My Troth* (New York: Harper and Row, 1975).

C. S. Lewis, *The Four Loves* (New York: Harcourt, Brace and Jovanovich, 1991).

John Piper and Wayne Grudem, *Recovering Biblical Manhood and Womanhood* (Wheaton, IL: Crossway Books, 1991).

Lewis Smedes, *Sex for Christians*, 2nd edition (Grand Rapids, MI: Eerdmans, 1997).

Paul Tripp, *Age of Opportunity: A Biblical Guide to Parenting Teens* (Phillipsburg, NJ: P & R, 1997).

Walter Trobisch, *I Married You* (New York: Harper and Row, 1971).

MONEY

Craig Blomberg, *Neither Poverty nor Riches: A Biblical Theology of Material Possessions* (Downers Grove, IL: InterVarsity Press, 1999).

Jacques Ellul, *Money and Power* (Downers Grove, IL: InterVarsity Press, 1954, 1984).

WORK

Lee Hardy, *The Fabric of This World* (Grand Rapids, MI: Eerdmans, 1990).

Leland Ryken, *Redeeming the Time: A Christian Approach to Work and Leisure* (Grand Rapids, MI: Baker, 1995).

NOTES

CHAPTER 1
A MAN AFTER GOD'S HEART

1. Harry Blamires, *Recovering the Christian Mind* (Downers Grove, IL: InterVarsity Press, 1988), pp. 109-110.
2. This is a paraphrase, not a quote, of Christian men's literature. Specific sources are available on request.
3. Jerry Bridges, *Transforming Grace* (Colorado Springs: NavPress, 1991), pp. 78, 75.
4. Bernard of Clairvaux, *On Loving God* (Kalamazoo, MI: Cistercian Publications, 1973, 1995), 7.17.
5. Ibid.
6. The encounter is a model of brevity and simplicity. "You are the man!" translates two Hebrew words. David's reply, "I have sinned against the LORD" translates three. And Nathan used just three more.
7. "God-fearing" probably denotes Gentiles who believe in God and accept the Decalogue, but not laws of food, circumcision, and sacrifice. Laws prohibiting close contact with Gentiles would force a centurion who became a Jewish proselyte to forfeit his post.
8. Of course, there is a kind of fear God always deserves, due to his grandeur and holiness (Prov. 3:5-7; Heb. 4:1 [where, contra some translations, the Greek says, "Therefore let us fear . . ."]).

CHAPTER 2
IMAGES OF MANHOOD

1. The subject of the sentence is masculine, but the conventions of Greek grammar, where masculine is the default gender, allow it to include both men and women.
2. For a secular analysis of this man, see Robert Bly, *Iron John* (Westminster, MD: Vintage Books, 1990), pp. 2-4.
3. Robert N. Bellah, Richard Madsen, William M. Sullivan, Ann Swidler,

and Steven M. Tipton, *Habits of the Heart* (New York: Harper & Row, 1985), pp. 3-26, 55ff.

4. David Brooks, *Bobos in Paradise: The New Upper Class and How they Got There* (New York: Simon & Schuster, 2000), pp. 25-53.

5. Christopher J. H. Wright, *Walking in the Ways of the Lord* (Downers Grove, IL: InterVarsity Press, 1995), pp. 120-122.

6. Bellah, et al, *Habits of the Heart*, p. 77.

CHAPTER 3
A MAN AND HIS MARRIAGE:
COMPANIONSHIP

1. The Hebrew reads, literally, "But as for Adam he did not find a helper suitable to him" (2:20). The active voice of the Hebrew verb, unlike the passive voice of the English translation, implies that someone, presumably Adam, is looking for a helper.

2. Ray Ortlund, "Marriage," in *Recovering Biblical Manhood and Womanhood*, eds. John Piper and Wayne Grudem (Wheaton, IL: Crossway Books, 1993), p. 101.

3. See James Olthius, *I Pledge You My Troth* (New York: Harper & Row, 1975), esp. pp. 19-42.

CHAPTER 4
A MAN AND HIS MARRIAGE:
THE THREE FACES OF LOVE

1. Lewis Smedes, *Sex for Christians* (Grand Rapids, MI: Eerdmans, 1976), pp. 92-93.

2. See my article "The Puritans, Sex and Pleasure," in *Christian Perspectives on Sexuality and Gender*, eds. Elizabeth Stuart and Adrian Thatcher (Grand Rapids, MI: Eerdmans, 1996), pp. 33-52.

3. In Aquinas's system, the idea that sex is evil does not necessarily mean it is sinful. If a husband and wife have relations for the sake of procreation, the act is considered evil but permissible.

4. See, again, "The Puritans, Sex and Pleasure."

5. Smedes, *Sex for Christians*, pp. 93-94. The next several paragraphs are indebted to Smedes, pp. 93-98.

6. Even on earth, Jesus was the supreme listener, His selflessness giving a singular focus on others so as to hear them. Yes, Jesus' divine prerogatives enabled Him to read people's thoughts (Matt. 9:4; 12:25; Luke 6:8; 7:39-40; 9:47; John 2:25), but He did not always use the prerogatives of deity (see Matt. 24:36).

CHAPTER 5
A MAN AND HIS CHILDREN

1. The Bible often compares God to a father: Isa. 9:6; 63:16; 64:8; Jer. 3:19; 31:9; Hos. 11:1; Mal. 1:6; John 1:12; Rom. 8:14-17; Gal. 3:26.

2. Scripture repeats this often, underscoring its centrality (Num. 14:18; Neh. 9:17; Ps. 86:15; 103:7-13; Joel 2:13; Jon. 4:2).

3. On God's justice and mercy, see Millard Erickson, *Christian Theology* (Grand Rapids, MI: Baker, 1983-1985), pp. 265-267, 297-298; Charles Hodge, *Systematic Theology*, Vol. 1 (Grand Rapids, MI: Eerdmans, 1975), pp. 367-374.

4. Even God's omnipotence and omniscience are germane. Pondering God's omnipotence, we recognize the limits of our power. His omniscience reminds us how hard it is to know ourselves or our children.

5. Micah literally reads, "They have told you, O man . . ." "They" refers to the Law and the Prophets, who agree that these points summarize God's will.

6. See also chapter 3 of this book and James Olthius, *I Pledge You My Troth* (New York: Harper & Row, 1975), pp. 20-23.

7. See Gary Smalley, *The Key to Your Child's Heart* (Nashville: Word, 1992), pp. 49-58.

CHAPTER 6
A MAN AND HIS FRIENDS

1. There are many articles, book chapters, and popular treatises on friendship, but few sustained theological treatments of the subject. See *Spiritual Friendship* by Aelred of Rievaulx (twelfth century), *Discourse of the Nature, Offices and Measures of Friendship* by Jeremy Taylor (seventeenth century), and *The Art of Being a Good Friend* by Hugh Black (twentieth century; Manchester, NH: Sophia Institute Press, 1999). Popular books today include Dee Brestin's *Friendships of Women* and Em Griffin's *Making Friends*.

2. Em Griffin, *Making Friends* (Downers Grove, IL: InterVarsity Press, 1987) pp. 142-158, 206. Griffin repeatedly mentions that friends enhance self-esteem before asking if his claim leaves readers uneasy (p. 206). Griffin is lucid but more a psychologist and communication theorist than a theologian.

3. Ibid., p. 153.

4. Ibid., p. 206.

5. C. S. Lewis, *The Four Loves* (New York: Harcourt, Brace and World, 1960), pp. 114-124. Some analysts think certain corporations transfer

executives regularly to prevent them from developing friendships that could inhibit loyalty to the firm.

6. David and his mighty men (2 Sam. 23:15-17), Elijah and Elisha (2 Kings 2:1-12), and Elisha and the Shunammite (2 Kings 4:8-37) may be additional models. Paul may also hint at friendships when he greets nearly thirty Roman believers by name, singling out Epenetus, Ampliatus, Stachys, and Rufus' mother among others (Rom. 16:3-16; cf. 1 Cor. 16:15-17; Col 4:9-15). More important, among all His disciples, Jesus chose twelve as his "friends" (John 15:13-15). And within the Twelve, the favored three shared the glory of the Transfiguration and the shame of Gethsemane.

7. C. S. Lewis, *The Four Loves*, p. 96. The next paragraph is loosely indebted to Lewis, pp. 90-105.

8. See Dee Brestin, *The Friendships of Women* (Wheaton, IL: Victor Books, 1989).

9. Of course, women unwittingly fall into friendships too. Susan Philips calls them "kitchen friendships" in "The Practices of Friendship," *Radix*, 23:4 (1995), p. 5.

10. This typology modifies one proposed by Jack Balswick, *Men at the Crossroads* (Downers Grove, IL: InterVarsity Press, 1992), pp. 177-184. His typology includes Good Ol' Boys, Locker-room boys, Sidekicks-topkicks, and Mentors-novices.

11. If one friend has an area of needed expertise, perhaps they could discuss personal subjects. Again, the friendship between the two men and the two women should ordinarily be primary, though one can think of exceptions. I want to urge caution without specifying legalistic rules.

CHAPTER 7
A MAN AND HIS WORK

1. Studs Terkel, *Working* (New York, Avon, 1972), xxxiv, xxxii; Lee Hardy, *The Fabric of This World* (Grand Rapids, MI: Eerdmans, 1990), pp. 32-33, 38.

2. See Hardy, *The Fabric of This World*, pp. 6-16 and Leland Ryken, *Redeeming the Time: A Christian Approach to Work and Leisure* (Grand Rapids, MI: Baker, 1995), pp. 71-73.

3. See Hardy, *The Fabric of This World*, pp. 16-26 and Ryken, *Redeeming the Time*, pp. 73-75.

4. Hardy, *The Fabric of This World*, p. 27.

5. Ibid., pp. 45-51; Gustaf Wingren, *The Christian's Calling: Luther on Vocation* (Edinburgh: Oliver & Bond, 1958), p. 9-10; Martin Luther, *Luther's Works* (St. Louis: Concordia, 1962, 1966), Vol. 44, pp. 98-99; Vol. 45, pp. 330-333.

6. John Calvin, *Institutes of Christian Religion* (Philadelphia: Westminster, 1960), 3.10.6.
7. Calvin, *Institutes*, 1.16.3.
8. Calvin, *Institutes*, 1.2.2; 1.14.4.
9. The Greek term (*tekton*) we translate as "carpenter" in Mark 6:3 includes carpenters, stonemasons, and metalworkers. So while we should not think of steel girders, hard hats, or unsavory habits, Jesus was a construction worker.

CHAPTER 8
A MAN AS LEADER

1. Martin Luther, *Table Talk*, in *Luther's Works*, trans. Theodore Tappert (St. Louis: Concordia, 1967), p. 158.
2. There are two words for gentleness in the New Testament. Galatians (5:23) suggests gentle humility. Timothy here suggests gentle mildness.
3. If someone wants to read 1 Timothy 3:2 hyper-literally and demand that elders have one wife, then they should also require that elders have two or more children, since 3:4 says elders must keep their children in respectful submission.
4. The Greek, *henos andras gunē*, literally means "a one-man woman."
5. David Brooks, *Bobos in Paradise: The New Upper Class and How They Got There* (New York: Simon & Schuster, 2000), pp. 127-133, 264-266.

CHAPTER 9
A MAN AND HIS WEALTH

1. With two sons, the older inherited two thirds and the younger one third. But death and divorce complicated matters. Also, someone might have no male heirs or too many heirs (Deut. 21:15-17; Num. 27:1-11; 36:7-9).
2. Of the fifty-four Greek words, thirteen are "I," "my," or "myself," and he addresses himself five times.
3. Seven of the parables in Luke feature internal dialogue. Self-interest or self-promotion is prominent in five of them: 12:17-20; 12:45; 16:3-4; 18:4-5; 18:11-12. (The other two are 15:17-19; 20:13.)
4. Daniel Doriani, *Putting the Truth to Work* (Phillipsburg, NJ: P & R Publishing, 2001), chapter 6.
5. Eye and heart are used interchangeably here and in Psalm 119:10, 18 and 119:36-37.
6. The Greek idiom, the "evil eye" (*ponēros ophthalmos*) meant a greedy or stingy disposition (see Matt. 20:15; 6:22-23; Luke 11:34; Mark 7:22; Deut. 15:9). A good eye (*agathos ophthalmos*) is generous (Deut. 28:54

[Septuagint], 56). This analysis rests on study of word usage in the Greek New Testament and the Septuagint, the earliest translation of the Old Testament into Greek. See also Leon Morris, *The Gospel According to Matthew* (Grand Rapids, MI: Eerdmans, 1992), pp. 153-154; D. A. Carson, *Matthew*, Vol. 1 (Grand Rapids, MI: Zondervan, n.d.), p. 178; W. D. Davies and Dale C. Allison, *The Gospel According to Saint Matthew* (Edinburgh: T & T Clark, 1988), pp. 638-640.

7. The term *Mammon* denotes money or wealth, especially when it functions as an idol or a rival deity. The word probably originates from the Aramaic *aman* (trust), with the original meaning, "that in which one trusts"—a particularly suitable name for money as God's rival. See *mamonas*, F. Hauck, *Theological Dictionary of the New Testament*, Vol. 4, ed. G. Kittel (Grand Rapids, MI: Eerdmans, 1933-1974), pp. 388-390; Joachim Jeremias, *New Testament Theology* (New York: Macmillan, 1971), pp. 222-223; Leon Morris, *The Gospel According to Matthew* (Grand Rapids, MI: Eerdmans, 1992), pp. 155-156; W. D. Davies and Dale C. Allison, *The Gospel According to Saint Matthew* (Edinburgh: T & T Clark, 1988), pp. 641-642.

8. For a cultural analysis of money, see Jacques Ellul, *Money and Power* (Grand Rapids, MI: Eerdmans, 1984).

9. R. V. G. Tasker, *The Gospel According to St. Matthew*, Tyndale Commentary (Grand Rapids, MI: Eerdmans, 1961), p. 76.

10. Craig Blomberg, *Neither Poverty nor Riches* (Grand Rapids, MI: Eerdmans, 1999), p. 132. See note 41.

CHAPTER 10
A MAN AND HIS PLAY

1. Leland Ryken, *Redeeming the Time* (Grand Rapids, MI: Baker, 1995), pp. 118-119; Thomas Adams, *The Works of Thomas Adams*, Vol. 3 (Edinburgh: J. Nichol, 1861), p. 134.

2. Gary Warner, *Competition* (Elgin, IL: David C. Cook, 1979).

3. The phrase is from Carmen Renee Berry, *Are You Having Fun Yet?* (Nashville: Thomas Nelson, 1992), p. 43; but my discussion owes more to Robert K. Johnston, *The Christian at Play* (Grand Rapids, MI: Eerdmans, 1983), pp. 31-49.

4. Organized sports are not the opposite of disorganized sports. *Organized* means organized by adults, not children.

5. David Holmquist, "Will There Be Baseball in Heaven?" *Christianity Today*, January 10, 1994, pp. 29-30.

6. Ryken, *Redeeming the Time*, pp. 183-189.

7. Ibid., pp. 165-167; Josef Pieper, *Leisure the Basis of Culture* (San Marino, CA: Pantheon, 1952), pp. 51-60.

8. Apocryphal stories are shallow and demeaning to Jesus. Jesus was a normal child, so we assume He played; but we have no record of it. The Bible is the account of redemption, not the cure for curiosity.

9. Robert Stein, *The Method and Message of Jesus' Teachings* (Louisville: Westminster John Knox Press, 1994), p. 13; Craig Keener, *Commentary on the Gospel of Matthew* (Grand Rapids, MI: Eerdmans, 1999), pp. 551-552.

10. For example, when the Philistines capture the ark of the covenant, the statue of Dagon, their deity, keeps falling down (and losing body parts) as if to worship before God's ark. The Philistines have to prop him up again and again. See also the account of David feigning insanity in the court of Achish (1 Sam. 21).

11. Margaret Mead, "The Pattern of Leisure in Contemporary Culture," in Eric Larrabee and Rolf Meyersohn, *Mass Leisure* (Glencoe, IL: Free Press, 1958), pp. 10-12.

12. Jurgen Moltmann, *Theology of Play*, trans. Reinhard Ulrich (New York: Harper & Row, 1972), pp. 1-14.

13. Augustine, *Confessions*, 10:21-37.

14. Kevin Freiberg and Juckie Freiberg, *Nuts! Southwest Airlines' Crazy Recipe for Success* (Austin, TX: Bard Press, 1996), p. 202ff.

CHAPTER 11
THE GLORY AND THE MISERY OF MAN

1. Hebrews uses several Old Testament quotations to praise Christ. Passages the author cites from Psalms 2, 45, and 110 originally described men—Israel's kings, to be precise. But as he quotes lines about thrones, scepters, and rule over enemies, he applies them to Jesus. Thus the highest praise of mankind is never fully true of ordinary man. Rather Jesus, the God-man, fulfills the songs that praise mankind. This is especially true of Psalm 8. To be precise, Psalm 8 initially described Adam and Eve (mankind at creation). The grandeur of that psalm is unattainable for us, after the Fall, but Jesus steps in to take the role of man in glory.

2. See Dick Keyes's excellent book, *True Heroism in a World of Celebrity Counterfeits* (Colorado Springs: NavPress, 1995).

3. See Daniel Doriani, *Putting the Truth to Work* (Phillipsburg, NJ: P & R Publishing, 2001), Chapter 1.

4. Consciences become defective when 1) someone commits a sin repeat-

edly (especially if they are not caught); 2) the entire culture denies that an evil act is indeed wicked; 3) they deny that the Law binds them.

5. See David Wells's superb analysis of guilt and shame in *Losing Our Virtue* (Grand Rapids, MI: Eerdmans, 1999), pp. 129-141.

6. Ernest Becker, *The Denial of Death* (New York: Free Press, 1973), p. 4.

7. Dan Allender and Tremper Longman, *Intimate Allies* (Wheaton, IL: Tyndale House, 1995).

Scripture Index

General Index